Table of Contents

Part One
Using the Pastoral Circle

Part Two
Resource Essays: Perspectives on Justice and Poverty

Part Three
Activities about Poverty and Hunger

Part Four
Resources

PREFACE TO THE DO IT JUSTICE! SERIES

Our faith calls us to work for justice, to serve those in need, to pursue peace and defend the life, dignity and rights of all our sisters and brothers. This is the call of Jesus, the challenge of the prophets and the living tradition of our Church.

The social dimensions of our faith have taken on special urgency and clarity over this last century....Catholics have been challenged to understand more clearly and act more concretely on the social demands of the Gospel. This tradition calls all members of the Church, rich and poor alike, to work to eliminate the occurrence and effects of poverty, to speak out against injustice, and to shape a more caring society and more peaceful world.

As believers, we are called to bring our values into the marketplace and the political arena, into community and family life, using our everyday opportunities and responsibilities, our voices and votes to defend human life, human dignity, and human rights. We are called to be a leaven, applying Christian values and virtues in every aspect of our lifes.

A Century of Catholic Social Teaching
National Conference of Catholic Bishops

Welcome to the *Do It Justice!* series. The Center for Youth Ministry Development and Don Bosco Multimedia have created the *Do It Justice!* series to provide leaders in youth ministry with practical tools aimed at helping both younger and older adolescents grow in their awareness of and commitment to justice. *Do It Justice!* manuals are being developed on the topics of *Poverty, Human Rights, Environment,* and *Lifestyle Issues.* Each Justice manual will provide basic background material on the issue being explored, practical strategies for awareness and action, and suggestions on how to adapt these strategies to a variety of parish and school settings.

The *Do It Justice!* series is a natural outgrowth of the justice work of the Center for Youth Ministry Development. For the past half-dozen years, the Center has played a leadership role in *Global Horizons,* a national, collaborative effort aimed at making education and action for justice an integral element in the Church's ministry with youth and young adults. The *Global Horizons* project focuses heavy attention on establishing and training diocesan leadership teams. Each team, in turn, is charged with the task of developing a unique diocesan strategy to broaden the scope and number of justice programs with youth and young adults. As diocesan teams have taken root throughout the United States, there has been a growing call for effective learning materials to translate the Pastoral Circle (the awareness and action process central to *Global Horizons*) into practical programs for youth and young adults. The *Do It Justice!* series

POVERTY: DO IT JUSTICE!

Edited by
Thomas Bright

Contributors
**Mary Lee Becker, Felipe Salinas,
Susan Thompson, and James Schimelpfening SM**

THE WORLD OF
DON BOSCO
MULTIMEDIA
New Rochelle, NY

Do It Justice!

...ublished as a service for adults who love the young
and want to share the Gospel with them.

It includes awareness and action activities for social justice, background
essays, and resource listings.

Prepared in conjunction with
The Center for Youth Ministry Development

Cover art and interior illustrations by Jeanne Bright

Poverty: Do It Justice!
© 1993 Don Bosco Multimedia
475 North Ave., P.O. Box T, New Rochelle, NY 10802

Library of Congress Cataloging-in-Publication Data

Poverty: Do It Justice! / Thomas Bright, Editor
p.cm -- Do It Justice! series
Includes bibliographical references.
    1. Social Justice   2. Poverty   3. Religious life--youth
      I. Bright, Thomas.   II. Poverty: Do It Justice!   III. Series

ISBN 0-89944-205-6 $13.95

Printed in the United States of America

05/93   9 8 7 6 5 4 3 2 1

addresses the need of translating the Pastoral Circle into realistic program activities for younger and older adolescents. In the late summer of 1990, a core of youth ministry and justice education practitioners and thinkers met to respond to this need. The *Do It Justice!* series is a direct outcome of their meeting — a practical program for better integrating justice in Church ministry with youth.

Central to the *Do It Justice!* series are several fundamental beliefs:

* Justice is central to the biblical understanding of God. The God made known to us through the Scriptures and incarnated in Jesus of Nazareth is a God of compassion and justice.

* Because justice is central to God, it must, of necessity, be central to the life and ministry of the Church raised up in Jesus' name.

* Justice involves contemporary believers both in alleviating present suffering and in working to eradicate the causes of injustice and inequity in our society and world.

* Justice is an essential component in the Church's ministry with youth.

* Young people will move to involvement in action for justice if they are provided with an opportunity to understand the impact of injustice in people's lives and are offered concrete alternatives for effective involvement.

The format for each of the *Do It Justice!* manuals is identical. Each manual will include:

1. **An Introduction to the Pastoral Circle and Its Use (Part One).** The Pastoral Circle is a justice awareness and action process aimed at helping people to connect with a specific justice issue (Involvement), to understand its history and causes (Exploration), to measure their understanding and possible action strategies in light of Scripture and Church teaching (Reflection), and to live their lives differently in light of their new understandings (Action). Following the introductory essay on the Pastoral Circle, this section provides an overview of the book's activities and offers suggestions on how to put the activities together to meet the needs of different groups and settings.

2. **Resource Essays (Part Two).** Several brief essays providing background material for the teacher or group leader on the issue being explored are included in this section. The information provided in this section is additional to material used as part of planned program activities.

3. **Justice Awareness and Action Activities (Part Three).** Using the Pastoral Circle as its basic framework, this section offers 8-12 different approaches to each of the steps in the Circle. The introduction to each step offers practical suggestions on how to get the most from each activity. The activities have been selected and designed to provide a range of approaches and strategies.

4. **Resource Listing (Part Four).** This section provides listings of readings, videos, and organizations created to respond to the justice need being explored. It serves as a source for future awareness and action programming in the areas of justice and global awareness.

Whatever the justice issue you choose to explore, remember to *Do It Justice!*

ABOUT THE CONTRIBUTORS

Thomas Bright, D.Min., is a staff member of the Center for Youth Ministry Development where he serves as Coordinator of Global Horizons and the Center's justice ministry programs. He is co-editor of *Access Guides to Youth Ministry: Justice.*

Felipe Salinas is Coordinator of Youth Ministry for the Diocese of Brownsville, TX and serves as an adjunct faculty member for the Center's Certificate Program in Youth Ministry. Felipe maintains a special interest in the areas of music, youth culture, and catechesis.

James Schimelpfening, S.M., is chaplain and youth ministry coordinator for Daniel Gross High School in Omaha, NE. His prior missionary work in South America and ongoing involvement in immersion experiences in Appalachia and Mexico give a strong justice focus to Jim's work in campus ministry.

Susan Thompson works with the Columban Fathers Justice and Peace Office in Washington DC In addition to her efforts to promote a global vision and mission consciousness, Susan brings a strong focus on housing and women's issues to her work.

ACKNOWLEDGEMENTS

"The Pastoral Circle: A Guide to Analysis and Action on Justice Issues" by Thomas Bright and John Roberto is reprinted from *Access Guides to Youth Ministry: Justice* (1990).

"The Christian Vision of Economic Life" by the National Conference of Catholic Bishops is reprinted courtesy of United States Catholic Conference Office of Publishing from *Economic Justice for All* (1986).

"Three Levels of Reality" by the Justice/Peace Education Council is reprinted courtesy of the Justice/Peace Education Council from the *Infusion Handbook.*

"From One Earth to One World" by United Nations Commission on Environment and Development is reprinted courtesy of Oxford University Press from *Our Common Future* (1987).

"The Causes of Modern Homelessness" by Mark Grinker is reprinted from Food Monitor, Winter 1988, courtesy of *Food Monitor*/World Hunger Year.

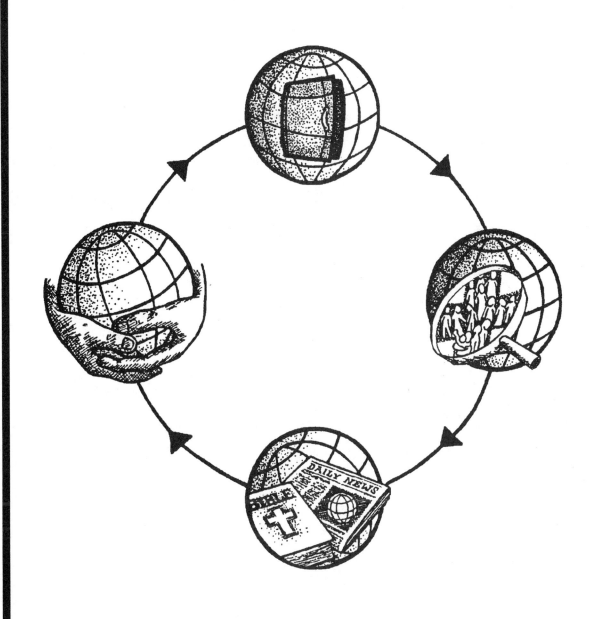

PART ONE

USING THE PASTORAL CIRCLE

THE PASTORAL CIRCLE:
A GUIDE TO ANALYSIS AND ACTION ON JUSTICE ISSUES

Thomas Bright and John Roberto

INTRODUCTION

A frequent temptation in service and justice programming with youth is to jump right from an experience of justice, especially one which touches young people personally, to action. Young people want, and need, to do something. While this approach may be of some help in responding charitably to pressing needs, it is less helpful as a response to structural injustice.

Structural injustice is not beyond the understanding of young people. In fact, it is a very real experience for many. Prejudice, discrimination, poverty, and need know no age limits. The challenge to those who work with youth is not to help them understand an abstraction called injustice, but rather to help them believe that they can do something about the very real social problems that touch their lives.

What leads young people, or any people for that matter, to action for justice? Several elements suggest themselves. First, they need to be connected — they need to be personally impacted by the issue, or at least feel how it affects others. Second, they need to understand the issue well enough to believe that their response will make a difference. Third, they need a sense of direction and hope, a sense that as large as a problem may be, it can be whittled down to size when people of faith work on it together.

The process of analysis and action used in this book involves young people in action for social change. It involves them too in analysis and reflection, a process aimed not just at immediate action, but at helping them understand the world in which they live and what they can do to make it a better place for all.

The approach to the Pastoral Circle used in this series has been adapted by the authors from the work of Peter Henriot and Joseph Holland in the hope of making their process more easily understandable and usable by youth and young adult groups.

THE PASTORAL CIRCLE

(Adapted)

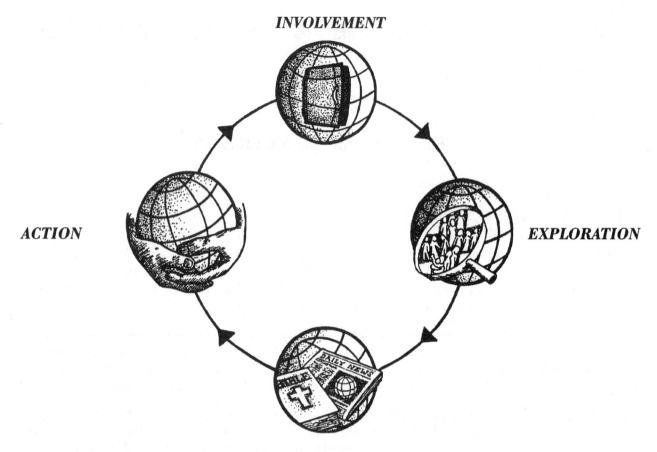

INVOLVEMENT

ACTION

EXPLORATION

REFLECTION

STEP ONE: INVOLVEMENT

The first step in the process — and the basis for any action — is *Involvement*. Through *Involvement* we connect with social issues and make them our own. *Exploration, Reflection,* and *Action* flow naturally from the lived experience of individuals and communities. Because we live not just independently, but as members of families, neighborhoods, school and work groups, towns, and nations, *Involvement* moves us beyond personal experience to reflect on the experience of the wider community. Because we are members of a church community, we experience and explore social issues from the perspective of Catholic social teaching. We try to feel and understand how social issues touch the lives of the poor. Getting in touch with what people are feeling, what they are undergoing, and how they are responding to the situations they find themselves in — these are some of the experiences that constitute *Involvement*.

The entry point for analyzing and acting on an issue may be:

→ an **event** — an experience of injustice;

→ an **issue** — hunger, poverty, environment, the arms race;

→ a **set of problems** — economic deterioration of a neighborhood, pollution;

→ a **question** — why does poverty persist in the richest country in the world?

Involvement, in some cases, may begin naturally with the experience of the group. The justice issues dealt with in this book may be part of the lived experience of the young people with whom you work. If so, the *Involvement* activities provide the young people in your group with the opportunity to express their feelings and thoughts about their experience. *Involvement* gives them the opportunity to ask how this same injustice is experienced by others.

Involvement, in many cases, however, will not spring from personal experience. In this case, the *Involvement* activities provide an opportunity to connect young people with the issue to be explored creatively. Good *Involvement* activities simulate the experience of injustice, helping youth "feel" the issue being analyzed, or expose them to what is happening in the local community, helping them to "hear" and "think" from a broader perspective.

Once they are connected with an issue, young people are ready to move to *Exploration*, to ask the "why" questions from an *Involved* perspective.

STEP TWO: EXPLORATION

The *Involvement* of individuals and communities in situations of injustice must be understood in the richness of all their relationships. *Exploration* is a means of widening our reflection on our experience to search out the relationships between values, events, structures, systems, ideologies. *Exploration* helps make sense of our *Involvements* by putting them into a broader picture and drawing connections between them. It goes beyond our immediate experience to probe the historical roots and future implications of events and issues and systems. The task of *Exploration*, the second step in the Pastoral Circle, is to examine causes, probe consequences, and delineate linkages rooted in the structural realities which condition our experience and limit or expand our freedom of choice.

For the Christian, *Exploration* will become a *habit of thought* which comes to expand our approach to all of our experiences. *Exploration* helps us become persons who habitually ask *Why* in the face of human suffering and injustice. We will always look for causes, relationships, structural realities in order to understand the plan for effective action for change.

The scope of *Exploration*, the resources needed, and the length of the process will vary from issue to issue. If *Involvement* (the entry point) is an event with which youth are very familiar, not much data gathering from external sources will be needed. We will not require a resource person to assist with *Exploration*. However, if we are trying to understand a complex social issue, or the way a whole system functions we may need a longer time period and some external resource persons to assist. The *Exploration* activities included in this volume offer a variety of approaches, some fairly simple and others more complex. Use the activities that best fit your needs and resources.

STEP THREE: REFLECTION

The third step is *Reflection* upon the issue in which people are involved and that they have explored, in light of the Scriptures, Church social teachings, the resources of our Tradition, and the lived faith of the Church community.

Faith is not just an intellectual process but a lifestyle as well. This step involves people in exploring what faith *says* about particular social issues. It involves them likewise in exploring what the faith community is *doing* about social issues and what *motivates* its response. *Reflection* should call forth not only an intellectual assent to faith but also a commitment to incorporate it within one's life. The witness of committed individuals can go a long way toward making *Reflection* real. The Word of God brought to bear upon the situation challenges old ways of thinking and responding by raising new questions, suggesting new insights, and opening people up to new action possibilities.

STEP FOUR: ACTION

Since the purpose of *Exploration* and *Reflection* is decision and action, the fourth step, *Action*, is crucial. Complex social issues seldom lend themselves to simple solutions. Social problems can seem overwhelming. But their very complexity makes it possible to approach action for change from many different angles. If *Reflection* helps people to feel part of a wider faith community committed to justice, then the *Action* step helps them to identify the particular role they can play in weakening and eventually destroying injustice. *Action*, whether individual or group, is always seen within a community context. It can be locally or globally focused, short term or long term. It can be expressed in a variety of ways. But if it is grounded in *Involvement, Exploration,* and *Reflection* it will be effective. At the same time that it brings about small changes in social problems, *Action* can produce major changes in the lives of those involved.

A response of action to a particular injustice brings about new *Involvements* which call, in turn, for further *Exploration*, *Reflection*, and *Action* — each time building on and extending previous insights and experience. The Pastoral Circle process is more like a "spiral" than a "circle" — leading individuals and communities deeper into action for justice.

Bibliography

Carey RDC, Loretta and Kathleen Kanet RSHM. *Structural Analysis. The Leaven Movement.* Dubuque: Brown-Roa Publishers.

Hofbauer GNSH, Rita, Dorothy Kinsella OSF, and Amata Miller IHM. *Making Social Analysis Useful.* Silver Spring: Leadership Conference of Women Religious, 1983. (8808 Cameron Street, Silver Spring, MD 20910)

Holland, Joe and Peter Henriot. *Social Analysis — Linking Faith and Justice.* Maryknoll: Orbis Books, 1983.

DOING JUSTICE TO POVERTY USING THE PASTORAL CIRCLE

The chapters which follow offer a variety of approaches to growth in awareness and action around the issues of poverty, hunger, and homelessness. The variations in focus, method, and session length make it possible to put the suggested activities together in many different combinations. Each *Involvement* activity, for example, could be followed by at least three or four different *Exploration* strategies, and each *Exploration* activity by another three or four approaches to *Reflection*. This variety provides a lot of room for creativity and for adapting the process to the unique needs of your ministry setting. **The Chart of Connections** (see page 9) lists some of the possible directions you can take as you journey with your group around the Pastoral Circle. As you choose the path that best fits your needs, you will want to keep the following thoughts in mind:

1. FOCUS

While all of the activities are designed to help young people touch the general issue of poverty, individual activities are most often focused on a particular expression of poverty, for example, domestic homelessness or hunger in the developing nations of the world. Include young people in the decision-making process as you choose a focus area. Work for a consistency in focus as you move around the Pastoral Circle. Help your group to see the connections between the activities you select.

2. METHODS

The activities selected for each step in the Pastoral Circle offer a variety of methods. While each assumes discussion, the path to discussion may lead you through creative writing, a video viewing, or team creation of a True/False quiz. Choose a flow of activities that provides a good mix of methods. Using a variety of methods helps keep the topic fresh, acknowledges the reality of different learning styles, and allows a larger number of young people to assume leadership during your group sessions.

3. RESOURCES

The resources with which you're working — personnel and finances, space and time — may lend themselves better to some activities than others. If, for example, your parish, school, or neighborhood has strong global connections, gathering a panel to speak on the international dimensions of poverty may be easy. In other locations, "resource strengths" may lie in easy accessibility to video resources or in a flexible schedule that allows ample time for visits to local agencies or service sites. Know the limits and strengths of your resources. Choose your focus and activities accordingly.

4. THE UNIQUE NEEDS OF YOUR GROUP

Diversity is a given in any grouping of young people. The age range, maturity levels and life experiences of the group you are working with will greatly impact both what you do and how you do it. The younger the group, the stronger its need for learning methods that are creative, varied, cooperative, non-competitive, well-organized, and connected with personal experience.

Although all of the activites listed in this book were choosen or designed with the needs of younger and older adolescents in mind, some will prove more effective with one group than the other. Activities that the editors think will be more effective with the younger, or older adolescents are marked accordingly in the introductory sections of the appropriate chapters. As you grow in comfort with and knowledge of your group, choose the activities and approaches that you think best fit their temperament and talents. In the end, you are the best judge of what they can do.

A brief **Overview of Activities** is included in the introductory section of each of the next three chapters. The **Overview** provides a quick look at the title, focus, and methods used in each activity. Activities more appropriate to younger or older adolescents are duly indicated as well. Used in conjunction with the following **Chart**, the **Overview** should be helpful in setting a direction for your journey around the Pastoral Circle. The **Chart** sets forth several possible directions for each *Involvement* activity. Others are possible; be creative! When you've settled on a tentative direction, read through the selected activities closely, confirming or changing your original plan. Then take your first step to *Involvement* in awareness and action on poverty.

INVOLVEMENT	*EXPLORATION*	*REFLECTION*
Homeless, USA I-1	Down and Out E-1 A Human Face E-2 Poverty Around Me E-4 Analyzing News E-9	Zacchaeus R-2 Implications R-4 Word of Witness R-5 Preparing R-6 Good News R-7
Profile of Poverty I-2	Down and Out E-1 A Human Face E-2 Poverty Around Me E-4	Lazarus R-1 But I Say R-3 Word of Witness R-5
House of Dreams I-3	Down and Out E-1 A Human Face E-2 Poverty Around Me E-4 Analyzing News E-9	Lazarus R-1 But I Say R-3 Implications R-4 Preparing R-6
Journey of the Blouse I-4	Mouse's Tale E-3 Home from Journey E-5 A Global Quiz E-7	Implications R-4 Word of Witness R-5 Beyond our Borders R-8
Banana Splits I-5	Mouse's Tale E-3 Home from Journey E-5 Anything-But-Trivia E-8	Implications R-4 Word of Witness R-5 Beyond our Borders R-8
Taking a Stand I-6	Mouse's Tale E-3 Home from Journey E-5 By the Slice E-6 A Global Quiz E-7	Implications R-4 Good News R-7 Beyond our Borders R-8 Pope for a Day R-9
Myths About Food I-7	Mouse's Tale E-3 By the Slice E-6 A Global Quiz E-7 Anything-But-Trivia E-8	But I Say R-3 Preparing R-6 Good News R-7 Beyond our Borders R-8
A World of 100 I-8	By the Slice E-6 A Global Quiz E-7 Anything-But-Trivia E-8	But I Say R-3 Beyond our Borders R-8 Pope for a Day R-9
Minimum Wage I-9	Down and Out E-1 A Human Face E-2 Poverty Around Me E-4 Analyzing News E-9	Zacchaeus R-2 But I Say R-3 Good News R-7 Pope for a Day R-9
Absolute Poverty I-10	Mouse's Tale E-3 By the Slice E-6 A Global Quiz E-7 Anything-But-Trivia E-8	Lazarus R-1 Implications R-4 Beyond our Borders R-8 Pope for a Day R-9

AN IMPORTANT NOTE:

The Chart of Connections does not list *Action* activities. *Ingredients of an Effective Action Response* and a special process for *Organizing Action Reponses to Poverty and Hunger* are included in the introductory section of the chapter on **Action Activities on Poverty and Hunger**. The chapter also offers over 100 practical approaches to *Action*. Read through the chapter before finalizing your plans to guarantee that the *Action* responses you choose are in keeping with the other steps in your journey around the Pastoral Circle.

USING THE PASTORAL CIRCLE ACTIVITIES IN DIFFERENT LEARNING SETTINGS

The Pastoral Circle lends itself to a variety of learning formats. The activities suggested in this book have been selected and designed to fit comfortably within both parish and school catechetical settings. By creatively choosing from among the available activities listed, the teacher/group leader should be able to put together a program ideally suited to the needs of his/her setting and schedule. The following program models suggest how activities designed around the four steps of the Pastoral Circle can be combined to fit three different learning formats: mini-course, day-long program, and overnight retreat. All three programs have been designed around the theme of homelessness to demonstrate how similar activities can be used flexibly in a variety of settings.

Weekend and overnight retreat programs have proven to be particularly effective vehicles for faith sharing and catechesis. An overnight retreat offers many of the advantages listed above in describing day-long experiences; it also allows more time for building community and a sense of trust. An overnight retreat program might look something like this:

OVERNIGHT RETREAT

DAY ONE

7:00 PM	Arrival and settling in
7:30	Welcome, introductions, house rules
7:45	Icebreaker
8:00	*Involvement* Activity: Profile of Poverty
8:30	*Exploration* Activity 1: Giving the Homeless a Human Face
9:15	Break
9:30	Prayer—Theme: Jesus and the Poor
10:00	Refreshments, games songs
11:00	Quiet time
12:00	Lights out

DAY TWO

7:00 AM	Rising
8:00	Breakfast
9:00	*Exploration* Activity 2: Down and Out in the USA
10:15	Depart for visit to homeless shelter or soup kitchen
10:45	*Reflection* Activity 1: Thy Will Be Done — A Word of Witness
	Explanation of what happens at the shelter, why it is needed, who it serves; tour of facility; meal shared with the homeless; return to retreat site.
1:30	*Reflection* Activity 2: Lazarus and the Rich Man
2:15	Break
2:45	*Action* Activity
	Brainstorming direct service, advocacy, change group strategies that can be done as a group following the retreat experience; initial planning.
3:30	*Reflection* Activity 3: Preparing and Praying
4:15	Prayer
4:45	Evaluation/debriefing and cleanup
5:30	Departure

DAY-LONG PROGRAM

A day-long program offers a unique opportunity to focus attention in a concentrated way on a specific justice topic. Given the extended time period, it is possible to include learning activities that are longer in length than normal or that involve bringing the group to visit local social service or ministry sites. A sample, eight-hour program based on the issue of homelessness could look like this:

9:00 AM	Welcome, introductions, sharing of "house rules"
9:15	Icebreaker/focusing activity

OPTION: BAG IT!

Prior to the event, ask the participants to bring with them a favorite record/tape/CD or something that speaks of how they see themselves. As an opening activity, give everyone a small trash bag, asking them to put into the bag their coat or sweater and the "piece of themselves" that they brought along. They can handle the bag in two ways: carrying it with them throughout the day wherever they go or finding a safe hiding place in the building where they can leave it. The catch: anytime an adult sees an unaccompanied bag it will be picked up and "trashed."

9:30	*Involvement* Activity: Homeless USA
10:00	Break
10:30	*Exploration* Activity: The Poverty Around Me

The presentation will be done by a panel and focus on the local homelessness. One of the panel members will be asked in advance to suggest advocacy strategies for the group's consideration.

12:00	Lunch

The lunch served will be exactly the same as that being served today at a local homeless shelter or soup kitchen. This will involve a bit of advance planning, but should prove worth it.

1:15	*Reflection* Activity: Lazarus and the Rich Man

Discussion should focus on drawing parallels between the Gospel message and the situation of the homeless locally.

2:00	Break
2:15	*Action* Activity: Advocacy

Briefly describe these two action approaches. Brainstorm possible action strategies for Advocacy. Working in small groups, have the youth write advocacy letters to the editor of the local city or diocesan newspaper, local legislators, parish members for possible insertion in the parish bulletin. Share the letters with the whole group.

3:15	Break
3:30	*Action* Activity: Integrating Spirituality and Justice

Brainstorm possible action strategies for integrating the situation of homelessness into our personal, group, and parish prayer life.

3:45	Prayer

Include: reading on Lazarus and the rich man, litany or prayers of petition focused on the needs of the homeless, offering of advocacy letters.

4:15	Evaluation/debriefing
4:45	Return "trashed" bags; use the trash bags to pick up trash within and surrounding the facility you have used.
5:00	Depart

MINI-COURSE MODEL

The mini-course format is adaptable to both parish and school settings. In a parish setting, mini-courses can be an effective way of providing program variety, integrating catechesis with other program components, and meeting the different scheduling needs of the parish youth population. In school settings, a mini-course model lends itself to the creation of quarter-long rather than semester-long courses, or to an inter-session approach which features short-term mini-courses as focused learning experiences between regular semester courses. This last approach allows for a variation in topics and teaching styles that may not always be possible within regular semester courses.

SESSION ONE:

Involvement
Brief introduction to the Pastoral Circle (10-15 minutes)
Activity: The House of Your Dreams (30-45 minutes)

SESSION TWO:

Exploration, Part 1
Activity: Down and Out in the USA
View video (45-60 minutes)
Assign task to be completed prior to next session: clip two articles or references to the homeless from newspapers or magazines.

SESSION THREE:

Exploration, Part 2
Discuss video using process described in the House activity. Share news clippings, referencing them to what has been learned about the structural causes of homelessness.

SESSION FOUR:

Reflection
Activity: Implications for Me and Mine (45-60 minutes)

SESSION FIVE:

Action, Part 1
List and briefly explain the eight possible action approaches listed in the chapter on *Action* activities. Note that given the topic of homelessness, several approaches seem to lend themselves well to an action response: advocacy, direct service, and support for change groups. Brainstorm possible action strategies for each of these action categories, trying to include both individual and group responses. Briefly discuss the merits and feasibility of each strategy. Decide together on one personal and one group strategy in each category area on which your group is willing to work.

SESSION SIX:

Action, Part 2
Working in small groups, complete/plan your advocacy strategy, for example, writing a group letter to your state or federal representatives. Plan for the direct service response that will take place at another time.

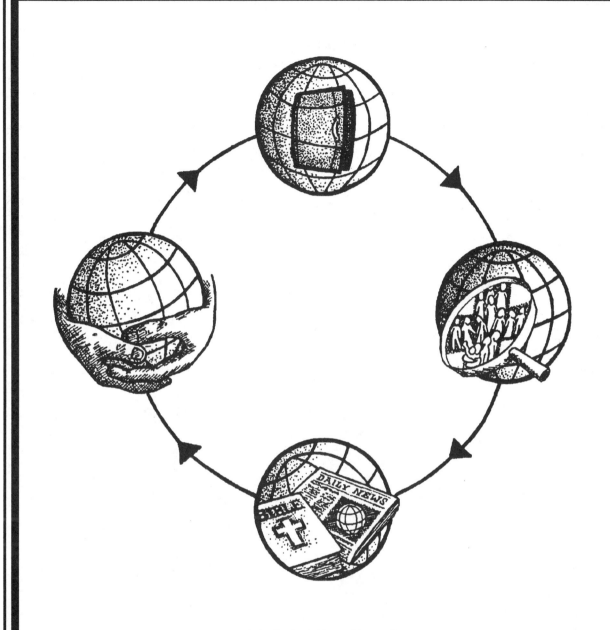

PART TWO

RESOURCES ESSAYS
PERSPECTIVES ON
JUSTICE & POVERTY

RESOURCE ESSAYS
Perspectives on Justice and Poverty

INTRODUCTION

Sprinkled through the activities in this book are nuggets of information that help put the issue of poverty in perspective. They range from statistics to Scripture quotes to essays touching on various aspects of poverty. The essays are a good source of information for program leaders, whether or not they plan to use the specific activities connected with the information. Among these essays are the following: *The Causes of Modern Homelessness* (E-2), *The Scriptures Speak on Justice* (R-4), *The Church Speaks on Justice* (R-4), *Basic Themes of Catholic Social Teaching* (R-7), and *The U.S. Economy and Developing Nations* (R-8).

The three articles which follow offer additional perspectives on justice and poverty. *From One Earth to One World* views poverty from within the broader framework of the world's economic and ecological situation. It helps us see the connections that exist between varied social concerns and the need for new approaches to deal with the world's problems in a consistent and effective manner. *The Christian Vision of Economic Life*, excerpted from *Economic Justice for All*, provides an overview of the scriptural basis for active Christian involvement in justice issues. The bishops emphasize that the economic concerns raised in the pastoral "are integral to the proclamation of the Gospel and part of the vocation of every Christian today" (60). Finally, *Three Levels of Human Existence* reminds us that justice needs to exist in all the ways we relate to others. The article offers valuable insights into the understandings and approaches that are necessary to effect change on the structural level.

FROM ONE EARTH
TO ONE WORLD

United Nations World Commission on Environment and Development

Interlocking Crises

Until recently, the planet was a large world in which human activities and their effects were neatly compartmentalized within nations, within sectors (energy, agriculture, trade), and within broad areas of concern (environmental, economic, social). These compartments have begun to dissolve. This applies in particular to the various global "crises" that have seized public concern, particularly over the past decade. These are not separate crises: an environmental crisis, a development crisis, an energy crisis. They are all one.

The planet is passing through a period of dramatic growth and fundamental change. Our human world of 5 billion must make room in a finite environment for another human world.

Economic activity has multiplied to create a $13 trillion world economy, and this could grow five- or tenfold in the coming half-century. Industrial production has grown more than fiftyfold over the past century, four-fifths of this growth since 1950. Such figures reflect and presage profound impacts upon the biosphere, as the world invests in houses, transport, farms, and industries. Much of the economic growth pulls raw material from forests, soils, seas, and waterways.

A mainspring of economic growth is new technology and while this technology offers the potential for slowing the dangerously rapid consumption of finite resources, it also entails high risks, including new forms of pollution and the introduction to the planet of new variations of life forms that could change evolutionary pathways. Meanwhile, the industries most heavily reliant on environmental resources and most heavily polluting are growing most rapidly in the developing world, where there is both more urgency for growth and less capacity to minimize damaging side effects.

These related changes have locked the global economy and global ecology together in new ways. Ecology and economy are becoming ever more interwoven — locally, regionally, nationally, and globally — into a seamless net of causes and effects.

Over the past few decades, life-threatening environmental concerns have surfaced in the developing world. Countrysides are coming under pressure from increasing numbers of farmers and the landless. Cities are filling with people, cars, and factories. Yet, at the same time, these developing countries must operate in a world in which the resources gap between most developing and industrial nations is widening, in which the industrial world dominates in the rule-making of some key international bodies, and in which the industrial world has already used much of the planet's ecological capital. This inequality is the planet's main "environmental" problem; it is also its main "development" problem.

The recent crisis in Africa best and most tragically illustrates the ways in which economics and ecology can interact destructively and trip into disaster. Triggered by drought, its real causes lie deeper. They are to be found in part in national policies that gave too little attention, too late, to the needs of smallholder agriculture and to the threats posed by rapidly rising populations. Their roots extend also to a global economic system that takes more out of a poor continent than it puts in. Debts that they cannot pay force African nations relying on commodity sales to overuse their fragile soils, thus turning good land to desert. Trade barriers in the wealthy nations — and in many developing ones — make it hard for Africans to sell their goods for reasonable returns, putting yet more pressure on ecological systems. Aid from donor nations has not only been inadequate in scale, but too often has reflected the priorities of the nations giving the aid, rather than the needs of the recipients. The production base of other developing world areas suffers similarly both from local failures and from the workings of international economic systems.

A majority of developing countries now have lower per capita incomes than when the decade began. Rising poverty and unemployment have increased pressure on environmental resources as more people have been forced to rely more directly upon them. Many governments have cut back efforts to protect the environment and to bring ecological considerations into developing planning.

The deepening and widening environmental crisis presents a threat to national security — and even survival — that may be greater than well-armed, ill-disposed neighbors and unfriendly alliances.

Globally, military expenditures total about $1 trillion a year and continue to grow. In many countries, military spending consumes such a high proportion of gross national product that it itself does great damage to these societies' development efforts.

The arms race — in all parts of the world — pre-empts resources that might be used more productively to diminish the security threats created by environmental conflict and the resentments that are fueled by widespread poverty.

Many present efforts to guard and maintain human progress, to meet human needs, and to realize human ambitions are simply unsustainable — in both the rich and poor nations. They draw too heavily, too quickly, on already overdrawn environmental resource accounts to be affordable far into the future without bankrupting those accounts. They may show profits on the balance sheets of our generation, but our children will inherit the losses. We borrow environmental capital from future generations with no intention or prospect of repaying. They may damn us for our spendthrift ways, but they can never collect on our debt to them. We act as we do because we can get away with it: future generations do not vote; they have no political or financial power; they cannot challenge our decisions.

But the results of the present profligacy are rapidly closing the options for future generations.

Sustainable Development

Humanity has the ability to make development sustainable — to ensure that it meets the needs of the present without compromising the ability of future generations to meet their own needs. The concept of sustainable development does imply limits — not absolute limits but limitations imposed by the present state of technology and social organization on environmental resources and by the ability of the biosphere to absorb the effects of human activities. But technology and social organization can be both managed and improved to make way for a new era of economic growth. The Commission believes that widespread poverty is no longer inevitable. Poverty is not only an evil in itself, but sustainable development requires meeting the basic needs of all and extending to all the opportunity to fulfill their aspirations for a better life. A world in which poverty is endemic will always be prone to ecological and other catastrophes.

Meeting essential needs requires not only a new era of economic growth for nations in which the majority are poor, but an assurance that those poor get their fair share of the resources required to sustain that growth.

In the end, sustainable development is not a fixed state of harmony, but rather a process of change in which the exploitation of resources, the direction of investments, the orientation of technological development, and institutional change are made consistent with future as well as present needs. We do not pretend that the process is easy or straightforward. Painful choices have to be made. Thus, in the final analysis, sustainable development must rest on political will.

A Call for Action

Over the course of this century, the relationship between the human world and the planet that sustains it has undergone a profound change.

When the century began, neither human numbers nor technology had the power radically to alter planetary systems. As the century closes, not only do vastly increased human numbers and their activities have that power, but major, unintended changes are occurring in the atmosphere, in soils, in waters, among plants and animals, and in the relationships among all of these. The rate of change is outstripping the ability of scientific disciplines and our current capabilities to assess and advise. It is frustrating the attempts of political and economic institutions, which evolved in a different, more fragmented world, to adapt and cope. It deeply worries many people who are seeking ways to place those concerns on the political agendas.

The onus lies with no one group of nations. Developing countries face the obvious life-threatening challenges of desertification, deforestation, and pollution, and endure most of the poverty associated with environmental degradation. The entire human family of nations would suffer from the disappearance of rain forests in the tropics, the loss of plant and animal species, and changes in rainfall patterns. Industrial nations face the life-threatening challenges of toxic chemicals, toxic wastes, and acidification. All nations may suffer from the releases by industrialized countries of carbon dioxide and of gases that react with the ozone layer, and from any future war fought with the nuclear arsenals controlled by those nations. All nations will have a role to play in changing trends and in righting an international economic system that increases rather than decreases inequality, that increases rather than decreases numbers of poor and hungry.

The next few decades are crucial. The time has come to break out of past patterns. Attempts to maintain social and ecological stability through old approaches to development and environmental protection will increase instability. Security must be sought through change.

This Commission has been careful to base our recommendations on the realities of present institutions, on what can and must be accomplished today. But to keep options open for future generations, the present generation must begin now, and begin together.

A Threatened Future

The Earth is one but the world is not. We all depend on one biosphere for sustaining our lives. Yet each community, each country, strives for survival and prosperity with little regard for its impact on others. Some consume the Earth's resources at a rate that would leave little for future generations. Others, many more in number, consume far too little and live with the prospect of hunger, squalor, disease, and early death.

Yet progress has been made. Throughout much of the world, children born today can expect to live longer and be better educated than their parents. In many parts, the new-born can also expect to attain a higher standard of living in a wider sense. Such progress provides hope as we contemplate that improvements still needed, and also we face our failures to make this Earth a safer and sounder home for us and for those who are to come.

The failures that we need to correct arise both from poverty and from the short-sighted way in which we have often pursued prosperity. Many parts of the world are caught in a vicious downwards spiral. Poor people are forced to overuse environmental resources to survive from day to day, and their impoverishment of their environment further impoverishes them, making their survival ever more difficult and uncertain. The prosperity attained in some parts of the world is often precarious, as it has been secured through farming, forestry, and industrial practices that bring profit and progress only over the short term.

Societies have faced such pressures in the past and, as many desolate ruins remind us, sometimes succumbed to them. But generally these pressures were local. Today the scale of our interventions in nature is increasing and the physical effects of our decisions spill across national frontiers. The growth in economic interaction between nations amplifies the wider consequences of national decisions. Economics and ecology bind us in ever-tightening networks. Today, many regions face risks of irreversible damage to the human environment that threaten the basis for human progress.

These deepening interconnections are the central justification for the establishment of this Commission. We traveled the world for nearly three years, listening.

We found everywhere deep public concern for the environment, concern that has led not just to protests but often to changed behavior. The challenge is to ensure that these new values are more adequately reflected in the principles and operations of political and economic structures.

We also found grounds for hope: that people can cooperate to build a future that is more prosperous, more just, and more secure; that a new era of economic growth can be attained, one based on policies that sustain and expand the Earth's resource base; and that the progress that some have known over the last century can be experienced by all in the years ahead. But for this to happen, we must understand better the symptoms of stress that confront us, we must identify the causes, and we must design new approaches to managing environmental resources and to sustaining human development.

Symptons and Causes

Environmental stress has often been seen as the result of the growing demand on scarce resources and the pollution generated by the rising living standards of the relatively affluent. But poverty itself pollutes the environment, creating environmental stress in a different way. Those who are poor and hungry will often destroy their immediate environment in order to survive: They will cut down forests; their livestock will overgraze grasslands; they will overuse marginal land; and in growing numbers they will crowd into congested cities. The cumulative effect of these changes is so far-reaching as to make poverty itself a major global scourge.

On the other hand, where economic growth has led to improvements in living standards, it has sometimes been achieved in ways that are globally damaging in the longer term. Much of the improvement in the past has been based on the use of increasing amounts of raw materials, energy, chemicals, and synthetics and on the creation of pollution that is not adequately accounted for in figuring the costs of production processes. These trends have had unforeseen effects on the environment. Thus today's environmental challenges arise both from the lack of development and from the unintended consequences of some forms of economic growth.

Poverty

There are more hungry people in the world today than every before in human history, and their numbers are growing. In 1980, there were 340 million people in 87 developing countries not getting enough calories to prevent stunted growth and serious health risks. This total was very slightly below the figure for 1970 in terms of share of the world population, but in terms of sheer numbers, it represented a 14 percent increase. The World Bank predicts that these numbers are likely to go on growing.

The number of people living in slums and shanty towns is rising, not falling. A growing number lack access to clean water and sanitation and hence are prey to the diseases that arise from this lack. There is some progress, impressive in places. But, on balance, poverty persists and its victims multiply.

The pressure of poverty has to be seen in a broader context. At the international level there are large differences in per capital income, which ranged in 1984 from $190 in low-income countries (other than China and India) to $11,430 in the industrial market economies.

Such inequalities represent great differences not merely in the quality of life today, but also in the capacity of societies to improve their quality of life in the future.

These pressures are reflected in the rising incidence of disasters. During the 1970s, six times as many people died from "natural disasters" each year as in the 1960s, and twice as many suffered from such disasters. Droughts and floods, disasters among whose causes are widespread deforestation and overcultivation, increased most in terms of numbers affected.

Such disasters claim most of their victims among the impoverished in poor nations, where subsistence farmers must make their land more liable to droughts and floods by clearing marginal areas, and where the poor make themselves more vulnerable to all disasters by living on steep slopes and unprotected shores — the only lands left for their shanties. Lacking food and foreign exchange reserves, their economically vulnerable governments are ill equipped to cope with such catastrophes.

Growth

In some parts of the world, particularly since the mid-1950s, growth and development have vastly improved living standards and the quality of life. Many of the products and technologies that have gone into this improvement are raw material- and energy-intensive and entail a substantial amount of pollution. The consequence impact on the environment is greater than ever before in human history.

Over the past century, the use of fossil fuels has grown nearly thirtyfold, and industrial production has increased more than fiftyfold. The bulk of this increase, about three-quarters in the case of fossil fuels and a little over four-fifths in the case of industrial production, has taken place *since* 1950.

In recent years, industrial countries have been able to achieve economic growth using less energy and raw materials per unit of output. This, along with the efforts to reduce the emission of pollutants, will help to contain the pressure on the biosphere. But with the increase in population and the rise in incomes, per capita consumption of energy and materials will go up in the developing countries, as it has to if essential needs are to be met. Greater attention to resource efficiency can moderate the increase, but, on balance, environmental problems linked to resource use will intensify in global terms.

Survival

The scale and complexity of our requirements for natural resources have increased greatly with the rising levels of population and production. Nature is bountiful, but it is also fragile and finely balanced. There are thresholds that cannot be crossed without endangering the basic integrity of the system. Today we are close to many of these thresholds; we must be very mindful of the risk of endangering the survival of life on Earth. Moreover, the speed with which changes in resource use are taking place gives little time in which to anticipate and prevent unexpected effects.

The "greenhouse effect," one such threat to life-support systems, springs directly from increased resource use.

Another threat arises from the depletion of the atmospheric ozone layer by gases released during the production of foam and the use of refrigerants and aerosols.

A variety of air pollutants are killing trees and lakes and damaging buildings and cultural treasures, close to and sometimes thousands of miles from points of emission.

In many cases the practices used at present to dispose of toxic wastes, such as those from the chemical industries, involve unacceptable risks. Radioactive wastes from the nuclear industry remain hazardous for centuries. Many who bear these risks do not benefit in any way from the activities that produce the wastes.

Desertification — the process whereby productive arid and semi-arid land is rendered economically unproductive — and large-scale deforestation are other examples of major threats to the integrity of regional ecosystems.

Many of the risks stemming from our productive activity and the technologies we use cross national boundaries; many are global. Though the activities that give rise to these dangers tend to be concentrated in a few countries, the risks are shared by all, rich and poor, those who benefit from them and those who do not.

Little time is available for corrective action. In some cases we may already be close to transgressing critical thresholds. While scientists continue to research and debate causes and effects, in many cases we already know enough to warrant action. This is true locally and regionally in the cases of such threats as desertification, deforestation, toxic wastes, and acidification; it is true globally for such threats as climate change, ozone depletion, and species loss. The risks increase faster than do our abilities to manage them.

Perhaps the greatest threat to the Earth's environment, to sustainable human progress, and indeed to survival is the possibility of nuclear war, increased daily by the continuing arms race and its spread to outer space. The search for a more viable future can only be meaningful in the context of a more vigorous effort to renounce and eliminate the development of means of annihilation.

The Economic Crisis

The environmental difficulties that confront us are not new, but only recently have we begun to understand their complexity. Previously our main concerns centered on the effects of development on the environment. Today, we need to be equally concerned about the ways in which environmental degradation can dampen or reverse economic development. In one area after another, environmental degradation is eroding the potential for development. This basic connection was brought into sharp focus by the environment and development crises of the 1980s.

The heaviest burden in international economic adjustment has been carried by the world's poorest people. The consequence has been a considerable increase in human distress and the overexploitation of land and natural resources to ensure survival in the short term.

Many international economic problems remain unresolved: Developing country indebtedness remains serious; commodity and energy markets are highly unstable; financial flows to developing countries are seriously deficient; protectionism and trade wars are a serious threat. Yet at a time when multilateral institutions and rules are more necessary than ever, they have been devalued. And the notion of an international responsibility for development has virtually disappeared. The trend is towards a decline in multilateralism and an assertion of national dominance.

New Approaches to Development

What is required is a new approach in which all nations aim at a type of development that integrates production with resource conservation and enhancement, and that links both to the provision for all of an adequate livelihood base and equitable access to resources.

The concept of sustainable development provides a framework for the integration of environment policies and development strategies — the term "development" being used here in its broadest sense. The word is often taken to refer to the processes of economic and social change in the Third World. But the integration of environment and development is required in all countries, rich and poor. The pursuit of sustainable development requires changes in the domestic and international policies of every nation.

Sustainable development seeks to meet the needs and aspirations of the present without compromising the ability to meet those of the future. Far from requiring the cessation of economic growth, it recognizes that the problems of poverty and underdevelopment cannot be solved unless we have a new era of growth in which developing countries play a large role and reap large benefits.

The pursuit of sustainable development requires a new orientation in international relations. Long-term sustainable growth will require far-reaching changes to produce trade, capital, and technology flows that are more equitable and better synchronized to environmental imperatives.

The mechanics of increased international cooperation required to assure sustainable development will vary from sector to sector and in relation to particular institutions. But it is fundamental that the transition to sustainable development be managed jointly by all nations. The unity of human needs requires a functioning multilateral system that respects the democratic principle of consent and accepts that not only the Earth but also the world is one.

Overall, our report carries a message of hope. But it is hope conditioned upon the establishment of a new era of international cooperation based on the premise that every human being — those here and those who are to come — has the right to life, and to a decent life. We confidently believe that the international community can rise, as it must, to the challenge of securing sustainable human progress.

THE CHRISTIAN VISION OF ECONOMIC LIFE

Excerpt from *Economic Justice for All*
U.S. Catholic Bishops

28. The basis for all that the Church believes about the normal dimensions of economic life is its vision of the transcendent worth — the sacredness — of human beings. *The dignity of the human person, realized in community with others, is the criterion against which all aspects of economic life must be measured.* [1] All human beings, therefore, are ends to be served by the institution that make up the economy, not means to be exploited for more narrowly defined goals. Human personhood must be respected with a reverence that is religious. When we deal with each other, we should do so with the sense of awe that arises in the presence of something holy and sacred. For that is what human beings are: we are created in the image of God (Gn 1:27). Similarly, all economic institutions must support the bonds of community and solidarity that are essential to the dignity of persons. Wherever our economic arrangements fail to conform to the demands of human dignity lived in community, they must be questioned and transformed. These convictions have a biblical basis. They are also supported by a long tradition of theological and philosophical reflection and through the reasoned analysis of human experience by contemporary men and women.

29. In presenting the Christian moral vision, we turn first to the Scriptures for guidance. Though our comments are necessarily selective, we hope that pastors and other church members will become personally engaged with the biblical texts. The Scriptures contain many passages that speak directly of economic life. We must also attend to the Bible's deeper vision of God, of the purpose of creation, and of the dignity of human life in society. Along with other churches and ecclesial communities who are "strengthened by the grace of Baptism and the hearing of God's Word," we strive to become faithful hearers and doers of the word. [2] We also claim the Hebrew Scriptures as common heritage with our Jewish brothers and sisters, and we join with them in the quest for an economic life worthy of the divine revelation we share.

A. BIBLICAL PERSPECTIVES

30. The fundamental conviction of our faith is that human life is fulfilled in the knowledge and love of the living God in communion with others. The Sacred Scriptures offer guidance so that men and women may enter into full communion with God and with each other and witness to God's saving acts. We discover there a God who is creator of heaven and earth and of the human family. Though our first parents reject the God who created them, God does not abandon them, but from Abraham and Sarah forms a people of promise. When this people is enslaved in an alien land, God delivers them and makes a covenant with them in which they are summoned to be faithful to the *torah* or sacred teaching. The focal points of Israel's faith — creation, covenant, and community — provide a foundation for reflection on issues of economic and social justice.

Created in God's Image

31. After the exile, when Israel combined its traditions into a written *torah*, it prefaced its history as a people with the story of the creation of all peoples and of the whole world by the same God who created

them as a nation (Gn 1-11). God is the creator of heaven and earth (Gn 14:19-22; Is 40:28; 45:18); creation proclaims God's glory (Ps 89:6-12); and is "very good" (Gn 1:31). Fruitful harvests, bountiful flocks, a loving family are God's blessings on those who heed God's Word. Such is the joyful refrain that echoes throughout the Bible. One legacy of this theology of creation is the conviction that no dimension of human life lies beyond God's care and concern. God is present to creation, and creative engagement with God's handiwork is itself reverence for God.

32. At the summit of creation stands the creation of man and woman, made in God's image (Gn 1:26-27). *As such every human being possesses an inalienable dignity that stamps human existence prior to any division into races or nations and prior to human labor and human achievement* (Gn 4-11). Men and women are also to share in the creative activity of God. They are to be fruitful, to care for the earth (Gn 2:15), and to have "dominion" over it (Gn 1:28), which means they are "to govern the world in holiness and justice and to render judgment in integrity of heart" (Ws 9:3). Creation is a gift; women and men are to be faithful stewards in caring for the earth. They can justly consider that by their labor they are unfolding the Creator's work. [3]

33. The narratives of Genesis 1-11 also portray the origin of the strife and suffering that mar the world. Though created to enjoy intimacy with God and the fruits of the earth, Adam and Even disrupted God's design by trying to live independently of God through a denial of their status as creatures. They turned away from God and gave to God's creation the obedience due to God alone. For this reason the prime sin in so much of the biblical tradition is idolatry: service of the creature rather than of the creation (Rm 1:25), and the attempt to overturn creation by making God in human likeness. The Bible castigates not only the worship of idols, but also manifestations of idolatry, such as the quest for unrestrained power and the desire for great wealth (Is 40:12-20; 44:1-20; Ws 13:1-14:31; Col 3:5, "the greed that is idolatry"). The sin of our first parents had other consequences as well. Alienation from God pits brother against brother (Gn 4:8-16), in a cycle of war and vengeance (Gn 4:22-23). Sin and evil abound, and the primeval history culminates with another assault of the heavens, this time ending in a babble of tongues scattered over the face of the earth (Gn 11:1-9). Sin simultaneously alienates human beings from God and shatters the solidarity of the human community. Yet this reign of sin is not the final word. The primeval history is followed by the call of Abraham, a man of faith, who was to be the bearer of the promise to many nations (Gn 12:1-4). Throughout the Bible we find this struggle between sin and repentance. God's judgment on evil is followed by God's seeking out a sinful people.

34. The biblical vision of creation has provided one of the most enduring legacies of Church teaching. To stand before God as the creator is to respect God's creation, both the world of nature and of human history. *From the patristic period to the present, the Church has affirmed that misuse of the world's resources or appropriation of them by a minority of the world's population betrays the gift of creation since "whatever belongs to God belongs to all."* [4]

A People of the Covenant

35. When the people of Israel, our forerunners in faith, gathered in thanksgiving to renew their covenant (Jos 24:1-15), they recalled the gracious deeds of God (Dt 6:20-25; 26: 5-11). When they lived as aliens in a strange land and experienced oppression and slavery, they cried out. The Lord, the God of their ancestors, heard their cries, knew their afflictions, and came to deliver them (Ex 3:7-8). By leading them out of Egypt, God created a people that was to be the Lord's very own (Jr 24:7; Ho 2:25). They were to imitate God by treating the alien and the slave in their midst as God had treated them (Ex 22:20-22; Jr 34:8-14).

36. In the midst of this saving history stands the covenant at Sinai (Ex 19-24). It begins with an account of what God has done for the people (Ex 19:1-6; cf. Jos 24:1-13) and includes from God's side a

promise of steadfast love (*hesed*) and faithfulness (*'emeth*, Ex 34:5-7). The people are summoned to ratify this covenant by faithfully worshipping God alone and by directing their lives according to God's will, which was made explicit in Israel's great legal codes such as the Decalogue (Ex 20:1-17) and the Book of the Covenant (Ex 20:22-23:33). Far from being an arbitrary restriction on the life of the people, these codes made life in community possible. [5] The specific laws of the covenant protect human life and property, demand respect for parents and the spouses and children of one's neighbor, and manifest a special concern for the vulnerable members of the community: widows, orphans, the poor, and strangers in the land. Laws such as that for the Sabbath year when the land was left fallow (Ex 23:11; Lv 25:1-7) and for the year of release of debts (Dt 15:1-11) summoned people to respect the land as God's gift and reminded Israel that, as a people freed by God from bondage, they were to be concerned for the poor and oppressed in their midst. Every fiftieth year a jubilee was to be proclaimed as a year of "liberty throughout the land" and property was to be restored to its original owners (Lv 25:8-17, cf. Is 61:1-2; Lk 4:18-19). [6] The codes of Israel reflect the norms of the covenant: reciprocal responsibility, mercy, and truthfulness. They embody a life in freedom from oppression: worship of the One God, rejection of idolatry, mutual respect among people, care and protection for every member of the social body. Being free and being a co-responsible community are God's intentions for us.

37. When the people turn away from the living God to serve idols and no longer heed the commands of the covenant, God sends prophets to recall his saving deeds and to summon them to return to the one who betrothed them "in right and in justice, in love and in mercy" (Ho 2:21). The substance of prophetic faith is proclaimed by Micah: "to do justice and to love kindness, and to walk humbly with your God" (Mi 6:8, RSV). Biblical faith in general, and prophetic faith especially, insist that fidelity to the covenant joins obedience to God with reverence and concern for the neighbor. The biblical terms which best summarize this double dimension of Israel's faith are *sedaqah*, justice (also translated as righteousness), and *mishpat* (right judgment or justice embodied in a concrete act or deed). The biblical understanding of justice gives a fundamental perspective to our reflections on social and economic justice. [7]

38. God is described as a "God of justice" (Is 30:18) who loves justice (Is 61:8, cf. Ps 11:7; 33:5, 37:28; 99:4) and delights in it (Jr 9:23). God demands justice from the whole people (Dt 16:20) and executes justice for the needy (Ps 140:13). Central to the biblical presentation of justice is that the justice of a community is measured by its treatment of the powerless in society, most often described as the widow, the orphan, the poor, and the stranger (non-Israelite) in the land. The Law, the Prophets, and the Wisdom literature of the Old Testament all show deep concern for the proper treatment of such people. [8] What these groups of people have in common is their vulnerability and lack of power. They are often alone and have no protector or advocate. Therefore, it is God who hears their cries (Ps 109:21; 113:7), and the king who is God's anointed is commanded to have special concern for them.

39. Justice has many nuances. [9] Fundamentally, it suggests a sense of what is right or of what should happen. For example, paths are just when they bring you to your destination (Gn 24:48; Ps 23:3), and the laws are just when they create harmony within the community, as Isaiah says: "justice will bring about peace; right will produce calm and security" (Is 32:17). God is "just" by acting as God should, coming to the people's aid and summoning them to conversion when they stray. People are summoned to be "just," that is, to be in a proper relation to God, by observing God's laws which form them into a faithful community. Biblical justice is more comprehensive than subsequent philosophical definitions. It is not concerned with a strict definition of rights and duties, but with the rightness of the human condition before God and within society. Nor is justice opposed to love; rather, it is both a manifestation of love and a condition for love to grow. [10] Because God loves Israel, he rescues them from oppression and summons them to be a people that "does justice" and loves kindness. The quest for justice arises from loving gratitude for the saving acts of God and manifests itself in wholehearted love of God and neighbor.

40. These perspectives provide the foundation for a biblical vision of economic justice. Every human person is created as an image of God, and the denial of dignity to a person is a blot on this image. Creation is a gift to all men and women, not to be appropriated for the benefit of a few; its beauty is an object of joy and reverence. The same God who came to the aid of an oppressed people and formed them into a covenant community continues to hear the cries of the oppressed and to create communities which are responsive to God's Word. God's love and life are present when people can live in a community of faith and hope. These cardinal points of the faith of Israel also furnish the religious context for understanding the saving action of God in the life and teaching of Jesus.

The Reign of God and Justice

41. Jesus enters human history as God's anointed son who announces the nearness of the reign of God (Mk 1:9-14). This proclamation summons us to acknowledge God as creator and covenant partner and challenges us to seek ways in which God's revelation of the dignity and destiny of all creation might become incarnate in history. It is not simply the promise of the future victory of God over sin and evil, but that this victory has already begun — in the life and teaching of Jesus.

42. What Jesus proclaims by word, he enacts in his ministry. He resists temptations of power and prestige, follows his Father's will, and teaches us to pray that it be accomplished on earth. He warns against attempts to "lay up treasures on earth" (Mt 6:19) and exhorts his followers not to be anxious about material goods but rather to seek first God's reign and God's justice (Mt 6:25-33). His mighty works symbolize that the reign of God is more powerful than evil, sickness, and the hardness of the human heart. He offers God's loving mercy to sinners (Mk 2:17), takes up the cause of those who suffered religious and social discrimination (Lk 7:36-50; 15:1-2), and attacks the use of religion to avoid the demands of charity and justice (Mk 7:9-13; Mt 23:23).

43. When asked what was the greatest commandment, Jesus quoted the age-old Jewish affirmation of faith that God alone is One and to be loved with the whole heart, mind, and soul (Dt 6:4-5) and immediately adds: "You shall love your neighbor as yourself" (Lv 19:18; Mk 12:28-34). This dual command of love that is at the basis of all Christian morality is illustrated in the Gospel of Luke by the parable of a Samaritan who interrupts his journey to come to the aid of a dying man (Lk 10:29-39). Unlike the other wayfarers who look on the man and pass by, the Samaritan "was moved with compassion at the sight"; he stops, tends the wounded man, and takes him to a place of safety. In this parable compassion is the bridge between mere seeing and action; love is made real through effective action. [11]

44. Near the end of his life, Jesus offers a vivid picture of the last judgment (Mt 25:31-46). All the nations of the world will be assembled and will be divided into those blessed who are welcomed into God's kingdom or those cursed who are sent to eternal punishment. The blessed are those who fed the hungry, gave drink to the thirsty, welcomed the stranger, clothed the naked, and visited the sick and imprisoned; the cursed are those who neglected those works of mercy and love. Neither the blessed nor the cursed are astounded that they are judged by the Son of Man, nor that judgment is rendered according to works of charity. The shock comes when they find that in neglecting the poor, the outcast, and the oppressed, they were rejecting Jesus himself. Jesus who came as "Emmanuel" (God with us, Mt 1:23) and who promises to be with his people until the end of the age (Mt 28:20) is hidden in the most in need; to reject them is to reject God made manifest in history.

Called to be Disciples in Community

45. Jesus summoned his first followers to a change of heart and to take on the yoke of God's reign (Mk 1:14-15; Mt 11:29). They are to be the nucleus of that community which will continue the work of

proclaiming and building God's kingdom through the centuries. As Jesus called the first disciples in the midst of their everyday occupations of fishing and tax collecting, so he again calls people in every age in the home, in the workplace, and in the marketplace.

46. The Church is, as Pope John Paul II reminded us, "a community of disciples" in which "we must see first and foremost Christ saying to each member of the community: follow me." [12] To be a Christian is to join with others in responding to this personal call and in learning the meaning of Christ's life. It is to be sustained by that loving intimacy with the Father that Jesus experienced in his work, in his prayer, and in his suffering.

47. Discipleship involves imitating the pattern of Jesus' life by openness to God's will in the service of others (Mk 10:42-45). Disciples are also called to follow him on the way of the cross, and to heed his call that those who lose their lives for the sake of the Gospel will save them (Mk 8:34-35). Jesus' death is an example of that greater love which lays down one's life for others (cf. Jn 15:12-18). It is a model for those who suffer persecution for the sake of justice (Mt 5:10). The death of Jesus was not the end of his power and presence, for he was raised up by the power of God. Nor did it mark the end of the disciples' union with him. After Jesus had appeared to them and when they received the gift of the Spirit (Ac 2:1-12), they became apostles of the good news to the ends of the earth. In the face of poverty and persecution they transformed human lives and formed communities which became signs of the power and presence of God. Sharing in this same resurrection faith, contemporary followers of Christ can face the struggles and challenges that await those who bring the Gospel vision to bear on our complex economic and social world.

Poverty, Riches, and the Challenge of Discipleship

48. The pattern of Christian life as presented in the Gospel of Luke has special relevance today. In her Magnificat, Mary rejoices in a God who scatters the proud, brings down the mighty, and raises up the poor and lowly (Lk 1:51-53). The first public utterance of Jesus is "The Spirit of the Lord is upon me, because he has anointed me to preach the good news to the poor" (Lk 4:18, cf. Is 61:1-2). Jesus adds to the blessing on the poor a warning, "Woe to you who are rich, for you have received your consolation" (Lk 6:24). He warns his followers against greed and reliance on abundant possessions and underscores this by the parable of the man whose life is snatched away at the very moment he tries to secure his wealth (Lk 12:13-21). In Luke alone, Jesus tells the parable of the rich man who does not see the poor and suffering Lazarus at his gate (Lk 16:19-31). When the rich man finally "sees" Lazarus, it is from the place of torment and the opportunity for conversion has passed. Pope John Paul II has often recalled this parable to warn the prosperous not to be blind to the great poverty that exists beside great wealth. [13]

49. Jesus, especially in Luke, lives as a poor man, like the prophets takes the side of the poor, and warns of the dangers of wealth. [14] The terms used for poor, while primarily describing lack of material goods, also suggest dependence and powerlessness. The poor are also an exiled and oppressed people whom God will rescue (Is 51:21-23) as well as a faithful remnant who take refuge in God (Zp 3:12-13). Throughout the Bible, material poverty is a misfortune and a cause of sadness. A constant biblical refrain is that the poor must be cared for and protected and that when they are exploited, God hears their cries (Pr 22:22-23). Conversely, even though the goods of the earth are to be enjoyed and people are to thank God for material blessings, wealth is a constant danger. The rich are wise in their own eyes (Pr 28:11), and are prone to apostasy and idolatry (Am 5:4-13; Is 2:6-8), as well as to violence and oppression (Jas 2:6-7). [15] Since they are neither blinded by wealth nor make it into an idol, the poor can be open to God's presence; throughout Israel's history and in early Christianity the poor are agents of God's transforming power.

50. The poor are often related to the lowly (Mt 5:3,5) to whom God reveals what was hidden from the wise (Mt 11:25-30). When Jesus calls the poor "blessed," he is not praising their condition of poverty, but their openness to God. When he states that the reign of God is theirs, he voices God's special concern for them, and promises that they are to be the beneficiaries of God's mercy and justice. When he summons disciples to leave all and follow him, he is calling them to share his own radical trust in the Father and his freedom from care and anxiety (cf. Mt 6:25-34). The practice of evangelical poverty in the Church has always been a living witness to the power of that trust and to the joy that comes with that freedom.

51. Early Christianity saw the poor as an object of God's special love, but it neither canonized material poverty nor accepted deprivation as an inevitable fact of life. Though few early Christians possessed wealth or power (1 Co 1:26-28; Jas 2:5), their communities had well-off members (Ac 16:14; 18:8). Jesus' concern for the poor was continued in different forms in the early Church. The early community at Jerusalem distributed its possessions so that "there was no needy person among them," and held "all things in common" — a phrase that suggests not only shared material possessions, but more fundamentally, friendship and mutual concern among all its members (Ac 4:32-34; 2:44). While recognizing the dangers of wealth, the early Church proposed the proper use of possessions to alleviate need and suffering, rather than universal dispossession. Beginning in the first century and throughout history, Christian communities have developed varied structures to support and sustain the weak and powerless in societies that were often brutally unconcerned about human suffering.

52. Such perspectives provide a basis today for what is called the "preferential option for the poor." [16] Though in the Gospels, and in the New Testament as a whole, the offer of salvation is extended to all peoples, Jesus takes the side of those most in need, physically and spiritually. The example of Jesus poses a number of challenges to the contemporary Church. It imposes a prophetic mandate to speak for those who have no one to speak for them, to be a defender to the defenseless—who in biblical terms are the poor. It also demands a compassionate vision that enables the Church to see things from the side of the poor and powerless and to assess lifestyle, policies, and social institutions in terms of their impact on the poor. It summons the Church also to be an instrument in assisting people to experience the liberating power of God in their own lives so that they may respond to the Gospel in freedom and in dignity. Finally, and most radically, it calls for an emptying of self, both individually and corporately, that allows the Church to experience the power of God in the midst of poverty and powerlessness.

A Community of Hope

53. The biblical vision of creation, covenant, and community, as well as the summons to discipleship, unfolds under the tension between promise and fulfillment. The whole Bible is spanned by the narratives of the first creation (Gn 1-3) and the vision of a restored creation at the end of history (Rv 21:1-4). Just as creation tells us that God's desire was one of wholeness and unity between God and the human family and within this family itself, the images of a new creation give hope that enmity and hatred will cease and justice and peace will reign (Is 11:4-6; 25:1-8). Human life unfolds "between the times," the time of the first creation and that of a restored creation (Rm 8:18-25). Although the ultimate realization of God's plan lies in the future, Christians in union with all people of good will are summoned to shape history in the image of God's creative design, and in response to the reign of God proclaimed and embodied by Jesus.

54. A Christian is a member of a new community, "God's own people" (1 P 2:9-10), who, like the people of Exodus, owes its existence to the gracious gift of God and is summoned to respond to God's will made manifest in the life and teaching of Jesus. A Christian walks in the newness of life (Rm 6:4), and is "a new creation; the old has passed away, the new has come" (2 Co 5:17). This new creation in Christ proclaims that God's creative love is constantly at work, offers sinners forgiveness, and reconciles a broken world. Our action on behalf of justice in our world proceeds from the conviction that, despite the power of injustice and violence, life has been fundamentally changed by the entry of the Word made flesh into human history.

55. Christian communities that commit themselves to solidarity with those suffering and to confrontation with those attitudes and ways of acting which institutionalize injustice, will themselves experience the power and presence of Christ. They will embody in their lives the values of the new creation while they labor under the old. The quest for economic and social justice will always combine hope and realism and must be renewed by every generation. It involves diagnosing those situations that continue to alienate the world from God's creative love as well as presenting hopeful alternatives that arise from living in a renewed creation. This quest arises from faith and is sustained by hope as it seeks to speak to a broken world of God's justice and loving kindness.

A Living Tradition

56. Our reflection on U.S. economic life today must be rooted in this biblical vision of the kingdom and discipleship, but it must also be shaped by the rich and complex tradition of Catholic life and thought. Throughout its history, the Christian community has listened to the words of Scripture and sought to enact them in the midst of daily life in very different historical and cultural contexts.

57. In the first centuries, when Christians were a minority in a hostile society, they cared for one another through generous alms-giving. In the patristic era, the Church fathers repeatedly stressed that the goods of the earth were created by God for the benefit of every person without exception, and that all have special duties toward those in need. The monasteries of the Middle Ages were centers of prayer, learning, and education. They contributed greatly to the cultural and economic life of the towns and cities that sprang up around them. In the twelfth century the new mendicant orders dedicated themselves to following Christ in poverty and to the proclamation of the Good News to the poor.

58. The same religious communities also nurtured some of the greatest theologians of the Church's tradition, thinkers who synthesized the call of Christ with the philosophical learning of Greek, Roman, Jewish, and Arab worlds. Thomas Aquinas and the other scholastics devoted rigorous intellectual energy to clarifying the meaning of both personal virtue and justice in society. In more recent centuries Christians began to build a large network of hospitals, orphanages, and schools, to serve the poor and society at large. And beginning with Leo XIII's *Rerum Novarum*, down to the writings and speeches of John Paul II, the popes have more systematically addressed the rapid change of modern society in a series of social encyclicals. These teachings of modern popes and of the Second Vatican Council are especially significant for efforts to respond to the problems facing society today. [17]

59. We also have much to learn from the strong emphasis in Protestant traditions on the vocation of lay people in the world and from ecumenical efforts to develop an economic ethic that addresses newly emergent problems. And in a special way our fellow Catholics in developing countries have much to teach us about the Christian response to an ever more interdependent world.

60. Christians today are called by God to carry on this tradition through active love of neighbor, a love that responds to the special challenges of this moment in human history. The world is wounded by sin and injustice, in need of conversion and of the transformation that comes when persons enter more deeply into the mystery of the death and resurrection of Christ. The concerns of this pastoral letter are not at all peripheral to the central mystery at the heart of the Church. [18] They are integral to the proclamation of the Gospel and part of the vocation of every Christian today. [19]

Endnotes

[1] *Mater et Magistra*, 219-220. See *Pastoral Constitution*, 63.

[2] Vatican Council II, *Decree on Ecumenism*, 22-23.

[3] C. Westermann, *Creation* (Philadelphia: Fortress Press, 1974); and B. Vawter, *On Genesis: A New Reading* (Garden City, NY: Doubleday, 1977). See also *Pastoral Constitution*, 34.

[4] St. Cyprian, *On Works and Almsgiving*, 25, trans. R. J. Deferrari, *St. Cyprian: Treatises*, 36 (New York: Fathers of the

---

Church, 1958), 251. Original text in Migne, *Patrologia Latina*, vol. 4, 620. On the Patristic teaching, see C. Avila, *Ownership: Early Christian Teaching* (Maryknoll, NY: Orbis Books, 1983). Collection of original texts and translations.

[5] T. Ogletree, *The Use of the Bible in Christian Ethics* (Philadelphia: Fortress Press, 1983), 47-85.

[6] Though scholars debate whether the Jubilee was a historical institution or an ideal, its images were continually evoked to stress God's sovereignty over the land and God's concern for the poor and the oppressed (e.g., Is 61:1-2; Lk 4:16-19). See R. North, *Sociology of the Biblical Jubilee* (Rome: Biblical Institute, 1954); S. Ringe, *Jesus, Liberation and the Biblical Jubilee: Images for Ethnics and Christology* (Philadelphia: Fortress Press, 1985).

[7] On justice, see J. R. Donahue, "Biblical Perspectives on Justice," in Haughey, ed., *The Faith That Does Justice* (New York: Paulist Press, 1977), 68-112; and S. C. Mott, *Biblical Ethics and Social Change* (New York: Oxford University Press, 1982).

[8] See Ex 22:20-26; Dt 15:1-11; Jb 29:12-17; Pss 69:34; 72:2, 4, 12-24; 82:3-4; Pr 14:21, 31; Is 3:14-15; 10:2; Jer 22:16; Zc 7:9-10.

[9] J. Pedersen, *Israel: Its Life and Culture*, vol. I-II (London: Oxford University Press, 1926), 337-340.

[10] J. Alfaro, *Theology of Justice in the World* (Rome: Pontifical Commission on Justice and Peace, 1973), 40-41; E. McDonagh, *The Making of Disciples* (Wilmington, DE: Michael Glazier, 1982), 119.

[11] Pope John Paul II has drawn on this parable to exhort us to have a "compassionate heart" to those in need in his Apostolic Letter "On the Christian Meaning of Human Suffering" (*Salvifici Doloris*) (Washington, DC USCC Office of Publishing and Promotion Services, 1984), 34-39.

[12] *Redeemer of Man*, 21.

[13] Address to Workers at Sao Paulo, 8, *Origins* 10:9 (July 31, 1980): 139; and Address at Yankee Stadium, *Origins* 9:19 (October 25, 1979): 311-312.

[14] J. Dupont and A. George, eds., *La pauvrete evangelique* (Paris: Cerf, 1971); M. Hengel, *Property and Riches in the Early Church* (Philadelphia: Fortress Press, 1974); L. Johnson, *Sharing Possessions: Mandate and Symbol of Faith* (Philadelphia: Fortress Press, 1981); D. L. Mealand, *Poverty and Expectation in the Gospels* (London: SPCK, 1980); W. Pilgrim, *Good News to the Poor: Wealth and Poverty in Luke-Acts* (Minneapolis: Augsburg, 1981); and W. Stegemann, *The Gospel and the Poor* (Philadelphia: Fortress Press, 1984).

[15] See Am 4:1-3; Jb 20:19; Si 13:4-7; Jas 2:6; 5:1-6; Rv 18:11-19.

[16] See paras. 86-90.

[17] See Selected Bibliography.

[18] Extraordinary Synod of Bishops (1985) *The Final Report*, II, A (Washington, DC: USCC Office of Publishing and Promotion Services, 1986).

[19] Pope Paul VI, *On Evangelization in the Modern World*, 31.

THREE LEVELS OF HUMAN EXISTENCE

Justice/Peace Education Council

The following diagram invites us to consider reality as consisting of three levels:

(1) the personal — within the self or between the self and God;

(2) the interpersonal — the relationship of the self to all persons in the family, school, workplace, church, and neighborhood;

(3) the structural — the level of institutions, structures, systems, and patterns (economic, political, social, cultural, and religious).

Levels of Reality

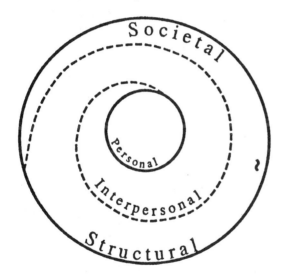

The swirling openness of the diagram is meant to connote the interdependent and dynamic relationship of the levels. The influence of structural level on our personal and interpersonal reality is a notion that has received little attention until recently. Generally speaking, many persons limit their analysis of issues and their actions to the personal and interpersonal levels. A number of contemporary social scientists and theologians have directed our attention to a systemic or structural level of analysis. They have asked us to examine the major systems of society to ascertain their impact on human dignity and community, on peace, justice, and the ecosphere.

While there is a growing consciousness among people about the effects of societal structures on our lives, this awareness is not yet widespread. Two pervasive mind-sets seem to militate against our grasping the implications of the effects of social forces.

Mindset #1 is often expressed as follows, "If only we are all good and kind to each other, then there would be peace in the world."

This reasoning suggests that an aggregation of good persons will always produce good results. We have only to recall that many good Christians owned slaves and never questioned the morality of one human being owning another. Indeed, growth in personal goodness is essential but it is not sufficient to bring about societal change.

Mindset #2 states the principle of home-first, "I know there are many national and international problems that need attention, but first I must put my own house in order and take care of the needs of those close to me before I can move into structural areas."

Personal striving for holiness is the work of a lifetime and action on behalf of justice and liberation of others is an essential component of that striving. And, this component is not, as some might think, a kind of post-graduate work. If it is not part of one's strivings, the basic message of Yahweh has not been grasped:

> This rather, is the fasting I wish; releasing those bound unjustly, untying the thongs of the yoke; setting free the oppressed, breaking every yoke, sharing your bread with the hungry, sheltering the oppressed and the homeless; clothing the naked when you see them and not turning your back on your own (Is 58: 6-8).

In truth, if we all waited for our perfect conversion before working to change the world, very little progress would take place.

One approach toward creating a better understanding of the levels of reality is to reflect on some terms commonly used. If, for example, we reflect on human needs and suffering, we see on the personal level the victim and we respond by acts of charity. Structural reality directs us to look also at the cause of suffering and to work to change it.

(*Dimensions of Justice and Peace in Religious Education* 15-16)

Distinctions among the Levels of Reality

[Editor's Note: The following chart offers additional examples of the shift in understanding and action necessitated by the movement from a personal to a structural approach to justice. In its simplicity the chart is a persuasive argument for a balance of individual and institutional responses to inequity and injustice.]

When moving from an understanding of personal and interpersonal reality toward one which includes structures as well, a double list of terms can help. To the concepts we have used at the personal and interpersonal level, ideas are added to help us understand the structural level.

PERSPECTIVES ON REALITY CHART

Personal & Interpersonal	Societal/Structural

Victims — **Cause**

When we look at human needs and suffering on the personal and interpersonal levels, we deal with the *victims*, and aiding the victim occupies our consciousness. The Church has been most successful at dealing with victims through works of mercy. Structural reality asks us also to look at the causes of suffering and work to change them, in addition to aiding the victims.

Mercy — **Justice**

We have always described our aid to victims in terms of virtues like *mercy*, *charity*, and *compassion*. When practiced on the structural level, these virtues are called *justice* and *peace*.

Conversion — **Influence/Power**

Change takes place on the personal level by *conversion* or *metanoia*, a turning toward a new realization. On the interpersonal level we seek to change others or to be changed ourselves by *influence*, mutual dialogue, and listening. At the structural level, change takes place through exercise of *power*.

Attitudes — **Organization**

When working for change on the personal or interpersonal levels, we work to change *attitudes*. On the structural level, we change organizations, systems, *structures*.

Personal Sin — **Social Sin**

Social Sin has been defined by Peter Henriot, SJ as a sort of institutionalization of *personal* wrong-doing. Greed, violence, domination become part of the culture, system, pattern or organizational reality.

Guilt/Blame — **Responsibility for Change**

When we see wrong in ourselves, we feel *guilty*. When we see others doing wrong, we often *blame*. When we see wrong on the structural level, we become *responsible* for change.

Programs — **Policy**

On the personal and interpersonal level, we seek to aid victims by *programs*. We address causes on the structural level by a change of *policy*.

Autonomy/Relationship — **Interdependence**

On the personal level, we strive for *autonomy*. On the interpersonal level, for *relationship*. On the structural level, this relationship is called *interdependence*.

Psychology-Humanities — **Social Sciences**

In studying and teaching about the human condition, we have used disciplines like *psychology* and the *humanities*, which deal with the personal and interpersonal realities. In trying to understand and interpret the human condition on the societal or structural level, we must add the disciplines of the *social sciences*: sociology, economics, political science, and anthropology.

(Adapted from *Infusion Leadership Workshop Manual*. Justice and Peace Education Council 1985. The Justice/Peace Education Council authors include Sr. Loretta Carey, RDC; Sr. Eileen Fitzmaurice, CND; Sr. Joan Hart, OSU; Sr. Kathleen Kanet, RSHM; and Sr. Rose Sheridan, CSJ.)

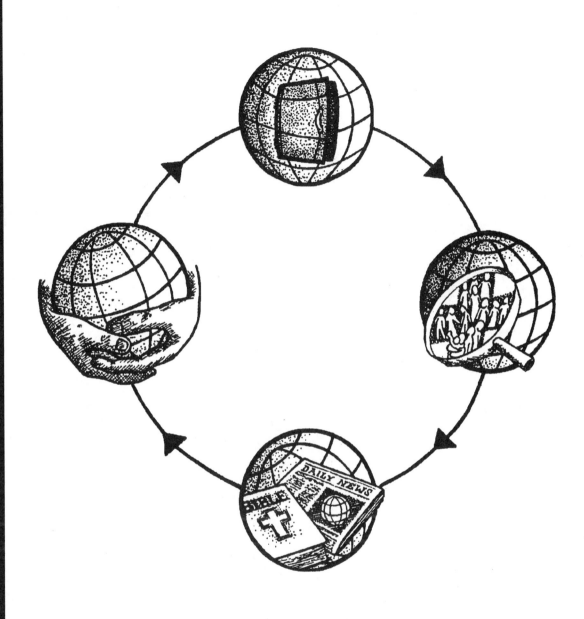

PART THREE

ACTIVITIES ABOUT HUNGER

INVOLVEMENT ACTIVITIES ABOUT POVERTY AND HUNGER

Behind all the statistics and stories on poverty and hunger stand real people. People like you and like me. People who share our strengths and struggles, dreams and disappointments. The more we come to see the people behind the statistics, the stronger our determination will be to change the situations that harm them. *Involvement*, the first step of the Pastoral Circle, helps young people connect with the issue being studied. They begin to see how it touches them personally, or reaches into the lives of others. *Involvement* provides the incentive needed to struggle with the difficult how and why questions. It provides the initial motivation for action to change the situations that hurt others.

The *Involvement* activities included in this chapter provide a sampling of different strategies and approaches to the issues of poverty, hunger, and homelessness. Use them as they are, or adapt them to fit the needs of your group and setting. If at all possible, involve the young people you're working with in choosing the specific issue to be studied. Poverty and hunger are viewed in this chapter from a variety of perspectives, ranging from local homelessness and the meaning of minimum wage to hunger in developing countries and the labor practices of multinational corporations. The more involved young people are in choosing the subject to be studied, the better their participation will be in all phases of the learning process. As young people grow familiar with the Pastoral Circle and experience the interconnectedness of social problems, it becomes easier to move them on to other issues.

CONDUCTING AN INVOLVEMENT ACTIVITY

*I*nvolvement activities are designed to engage both young people's hearts *and* heads around the issue of poverty, hunger, or homelessness. If the activities are properly prepared, well-conducted, and fully-debriefed, they should easily accomplish this goal. Here's how to do it:

A. Preparing for Involvement: In advance of the *Involvement* session, create an environment that lends itself both to the activity chosen and to the discussion that is sure to follow. Discussion flows more smoothly, for example, if people are physically comfortable and seated facing one another. Review the activity, gathering the materials needed and taking care of any other preparatory work well in advance of the session. If others are involved with you in a leadership role, review their involvement with them prior to the session. Audiovisual equipment should always be checked out in advance of the session and audio or video tapes reviewed.

B. Conducting an Involvement Activity: Identify the topic to be explored and provide a brief overview of the flow of the session. Provide the group with clear directions, timelines, and expectations using the Procedure notes built into each activity. Encourage all to participate fully. During small group activities, circulate among work groups responding to any questions they may have and encouraging them in their efforts.

C. Discussing/Debriefing an Involvement Activity: Prior to the discussion period that is built into or flows from the *Involvement* activity, tell the group how long the discussion will last, what the questions/issues will be, and the kind of response you're looking for. (Are you, for example, more interested in breadth of participation or depth of discussion around a single issue? In hearing where everyone is coming from, or in arriving at a common viewpoint?) Urge all group members to contribute actively to the discussion. Questions appropriate to the *Involvement* step include:

1. What is our personal experience of this issue or concern? Has any one of us lived in poverty (hunger, homelessness)? Have any of our family or friends experienced it? What was the experience like? How did it impact on the way we felt about ourselves? How did it impact on how we felt about others?

2. If we haven't personally experienced this need, where do our information and feelings come from? Can we point to any specific article, story, song, or video about the issue that struck us? What do we know, as a group, about this issue? What questions do we have?

3. What feelings do we connect with the issue? Why do people end up poor, or homeless, or hungry? Could it happen to you or me? Why or why not? What does it do to people? How does it make them feel? How does it make us feel?

4. What are we doing personally to change this situation? Are there ways we are already involved around this issue? How? Where?

5. How do we see the issue being dealt with in our local community? Does the issue touch us at all? How? Where?

6. What are the thoughts and feelings of the people in our local community, state, or nation about this issue? How are these thoughts and feelings shared? Do they have any impact on what we think or feel? Why or why not?

7. What is being done in our local community, state, or country to change this situation? Is it enough? Too much? Why?

During the discussion, attempt to keep the dialogue on track, summarizing or clarifying points as needed. When discussion is finished, thank everyone for their participation. Tie the discussion in with the session topic and give the group a glimpse of where the next session will take them.

The *Involvement* activities are briefly described below. Choose a topic and activity that are of interest to your group and start your journey around the Pastoral Circle.

AN OVERVIEW OF INVOLVEMENT ACTIVITIES

I-1 Homeless, USA *

Focus: Identifying stereotypical images and myths regarding homelessness in the US
Methods: Creation of poster illustrating the "typical" homeless person and offering
six warning signs of existing or impending homelessness; discussion

I-2 Profile of Poverty

Focus: Exploring the range of images and understandings of poverty and its causes held by group members
Methods: Word association exercise around poverty and its causes; discussion

I-3 The House of Your Dreams

Focus: Identifying current values and perceptions of need as they relate to the issue of adequate housing
Methods: Drawing and comparing floor plans for dream homes and simple living; discussion

I-4 Journey of the Blouse

Focus: Reflecting on global interdependence and the developing world's role in international business
Methods: Participatory activity tracing the resources used and people involved in making the clothing we wear;
discussion

I-5 Banana Splits

Focus: Exploring the justice issues involved in international agribusiness
Methods: Role play — negotiating for a share of the profits; discussion

I-6 Taking a Stand on the Causes of Hunger **

Focus: Identifying group assumptions about the causes of hunger in developed and developing countries
Methods: Creating a living continuum around the causes of world hunger; discussion

I-7 Myths About Food

Focus: Exploring popular myths and misconceptions about food production and consumption
Methods: Multiple-choice questionnaire; discussion

I-8 A World of One Hundred*

Focus: Sharing perceptions about world population; comparing lifestyles in developed and developing countries
Methods: Creating a symbolic representation of the world as we perceive it; discussion

I-9 Surviving on Minimum Wage**

Focus: Experiencing the challenges and frustrations faced by those living on fixed and inadequate incomes
Methods: Developing a monthly budget for someone working a minimum wage job; discussion

I-10 Living in Absolute Poverty

Focus: Understanding the impact of absolute poverty on the living conditions of the world's poor
Methods: Guided imagery experience; discussion

---

* These activities should prove particularly effective with *younger* adolescents.

** These activities should prove particularly effective with *older* adolescents.

Description of Activity:

Creation of a poster illustrating the "typical" homeless person and offering six warning signs of existing or impending homelessness.

Objective:

To identify stereotypical images and myths regarding homelessness in the USA

Time:

30 minutes.

Materials:

Newsprint, markers, *Homeless, USA* worksheet, pencils/pens.

Prior to the Activity:

Gather materials, duplicate *Homeless, USA* worksheet for distribution to individuals or small groups.

Procedure

1. Introduce the topic. Have the group brainstorm the sources of its information about and attitudes toward the homeless. Note that these varied sources provide different images of who the homeless are and how they got there.

2. Working in teams of 4-6, have the individuals share their images of the "typical" homeless person in the United States.

3. Using the *Homeless, USA* worksheet or a large sheet of newsprint, ask each team to draw a detailed illustration of a typical homeless person. At the bottom of the sheet, in the *Homeless Alert* section, have the group identify six characteristics of homelessness — indicators that could be used in picking the homeless out of a crowd.

4. Ask each team share its illustration and *Homeless Alert* listing. Discuss the similarities and differences between the various presentations of homelessness.

HOMELESS, USA

A typical homeless person looks like this:

HOMELESS ALERT/HOMELESS ALERT/HOMELESS ALERT

*Picking a Homeless Person out of a Crowd: List six key indicators
you could use to identify someone who is homeless.*

1. _____

2. _____

3. _____

4. _____

5. _____

6. _____

I-2 *PROFILE OF POVERTY*

Description of Activity:

Word association exercise around poverty and its causes.

Objective:

To explore the range of images and understandings of poverty and its causes presently held by group members.

Time:

15 minutes.

Materials:

Newsprint, markers, *Poor Because ...* worksheet, pencils/pens.

Prior to the Activity:

Gather materials, duplicate *Poor Because ...* worksheet for distribution to group members.

Procedure

1. Invite the group to join you in a quick, word association exercise. Share simple directions for the exercise — After you've introduced a word by writing it on newsprint, group members should call out the words, images, feelings, and thoughts they associate with the word — leaving enough time between responses for you to write their reflections on the newsprint.

2. Start the word association exercise with a neutral word or two, for example "spring" or "friendship." When the group is comfortable with the process, ask them to share their associations with "poverty."

3. Without commenting on their responses, invite the group to move beyond the word association exercise to a discussion of the causes of poverty.

4. Distribute the *Poor Because ...* worksheet, asking members to fill it out individually.

5. Form groups of 4-6. Invite participants to share what they listed as the primary causes of poverty, and why they chose those particular items. Ask a representative from each group to share the major agreements and/or disagreements that arose in the group around the causes of poverty. List the areas of agreement and disagreement on newsprint. Keep the newsprint to refer back to in later sessions.

Source: *Poor Because...* worksheet is adapted from *Economic Rights and Human Development* by Alyson Huntly, Jim Morin and Marsha Sfeir (Dubuque: Wm. C. Brown Company Publishers, 1984)

POOR BECAUSE...

Directions:

From the following list, choose the three responses you think best describe why people are poor:

People are poor because:

_____ they are lazy and do not work hard enough to earn what they need.

_____ they do not have work (unemployment).

_____ even though they work hard, they do not earn enough money to buy what they need (wages are too low).

_____ they do not have enough education or skills.

_____ they have too many children.

_____ they are discriminated against (treated unfairly) because of their color, nationality, religion, or sex.

_____ government ignores the needs of the poor.

_____ of illness or disease.

_____ they do not have enough initiative (people just sit back and wait for things to happen).

_____ no reason in particular, that's just the way the world is.

_____ there are too many needs in the world and not enough resources to meet them all.

_____ of natural disasters such as floods or earthquakes.

_____ there are enough resources in the world for everyone to have what they need but these resources are not shared fairly.

_____ too much money is spent on weapons and not enough on buying what people need.

_____ resources (food, water, land, energy) are wasted rather than being used for what people need.

_____ the current business system doesn't need as many workers.

_____ other reasons (list any you can think of).

I-3 *THE HOUSE OF YOUR DREAMS*

Description of Activity:

Exploration of housing needs through comparison of basic/adequate and dream/luxury homes.

Objective:

To identify current values and perceptions of need as they relate to the issue of adequate housing.

Time:

30-45 minutes.

Materials:

Newsprint, markers, colored pencils/crayons, home sales booklets or real estate sections from daily/Sunday newspapers, *House Rating* worksheet.

Prior to the Activity:

Gather materials, duplicate *House Rating* worksheet for distribution to group members.

Procedure

1. Introduce the topic. Using blank sheets of paper, ask group members to draw a simple floor plan of the house or apartment in which they live, labelling each room.

2. Using the *House Rating* worksheet, have them individually rate their homes.

3. Divide the group into teams of 4-6, providing each group with newsprint and markers.

4. Assign half of the teams the task of designing a dream house for a family of four. The home sales booklets and real estate ads can be used as resources in designing their ideal home and estimating its probable cost.

5. The remaining teams are assigned the task of designing a simple home that adequately meets the basic needs of a family of four. Home sales booklets and real estate ads can be used in designing the home and estimating its probable cost.

6. Have teams share their floor plans and price estimates. Lead them in a discussion of what "adequate" housing means in their city or town... in other places in the USA... in other nations of the world. See if the group can come up with any universal standards for adequate housing.

Δ On a scale of 1 (poor) to 10 (great), I think my house is a ____ because:

Δ My two favorite rooms in the house are

_____

and _____.

Δ The room I use least is _____.

Δ If you could improve your house in one way, what would you change?

Δ If you were building the "ideal" home what would it include?

Δ If you could only have four things in your house, what would be essential for you?

CHOOSE

Description of Activity:

Tracing the resources used and people involved in making the clothing we wear.

Objectives:

To help young people reflect upon global interdependence and the role played by the developing world in international business.

Time:

30 minutes.

Materials:

World map (Peters Projection Map — See Resources, page 135), string/yarn, thumbtacks, *Journey of the Blouse* narrative.

Prior to the Activity:

Post the world map in a location at the front of the room; duplicate the *Journey of the Blouse* narrative, cutting it into country strips for individual readers.

Procedure

1. Introduce the activity by having participants find a label in a piece of clothing they are wearing and identify where it was made. Explain that the group will be following the journey of one article of clothing, a blouse.

2. Select eight participants from the group and distribute one paragraph to each person from the *Journey* narrative. Have the person holding country number one read his/her paragraph. When finished, ask the reader to locate the country on the map and thumbtack the country strip to that point on the map. A long piece of string or yard should also be tacked to the map at this first location. Continue the story by having participants read their paragraphs and locate their countries or states on the map. Tracing the blouse's journey visibly by connecting the various points on the map.

3. After the last step in the journey has been described, ask for reactions from the group. What surprised them? Do they think the blouse's journey is different from that of most the clothes they buy and wear? What items, apart from clothing, take similar international journeys before ending up in their homes? What does the blouse's journey suggest about the relationship of our consumer products and the economy of the United States? What does the journey suggest about the relationship between the people of the United States and those of less developed countries around the world?

Source: *Journey of the Blouse* is taken from *Make a World of Difference* by Office on Global Education, (Baltimore: Office on Global Education, Church World Service, 1989) and used with permission.

Note: A poster of the *Journey* can be purchased from *Seeds Magazine*, 222 East Lake Drive, Decatur, GA 30030.

JOURNEY OF THE BLOUSE:
A NARRATIVE

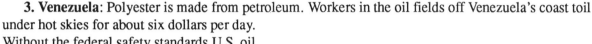

1. El Salvador: Workers in this war-torn province harvest cotton on long, hot days. They earn about two dollars a day. The government has diverted millions of pesos from health and literacy programs into weapons.

2. South Carolina: The cotton is ginned and shipped to South Carolina by a U.S. corporation whose bargaining position vis-a-vis the Salvadoran landowner is ridiculously strong. In South Carolina, the cotton is sold to the United States' largest textile company for its spinning mills.

3. Venezuela: Polyester is made from petroleum. Workers in the oil fields off Venezuela's coast toil under hot skies for about six dollars per day. Without the federal safety standards U.S. oil workers have won, the job is dangerous and disfiguring accidents are not uncommon. After pumping and refining the oil, the Venezuelan state company sells it to a U.S. petroleum company, which controls processing, marketing, and final distribution of petroleum, the most lucrative parts of the production chain.

4. Trinidad: This same U.S. oil company drops the oil off at one of its refineries in Trinidad and Tobago. Here, in conditions as dangerous and unhealthy as Venezuela, refined petroleum is further processed into petrochemicals.

5. New Jersey: Our U.S. oil company now ships the petrochemicals to a chemical factory in New Jersey where they are propelled through machines and emerge as miles of continuous filament.

6. North Carolina: The polyester filament is taken to North Carolina, site of low-wage textile mills where, on high-powered looms, it is combined with the cotton yarn from the plant in South Carolina. The filament and yard are woven into long sheets of fabric ready for the cutting table. At this stage a U.S. retailer chain that eventually sells the blouse, buys the cloth.

7. Haiti: The cloth is transported to small, Haitian-owned and Haitian-run sweatshops. Women being paid by the piece earn about three dollars a day. They bend over sewing machines for long hours stitching seams. They have no union and talk about creating one may result in dismissal or worse.

8. New York: The finished blouses leave the Third World for the final time and arrive in New York where they are sealed in plastic and sent to mail order buyers around the country.

I-5 *BANANA SPLITS*

Description of Activity:

Using the division of a banana to explore the issue of world trade and the rights of local workers.

Objectives:

To expand group members' understanding of world trade and help them identify with growers and producers in the U.S. and internationally.

Time:

30 minutes.

Materials:

Newsprint/Posterboard, markers, paper, pencils, bananas, knives.

Prior to the Activity:

Gather materials; prepare a wall chart of the *Banana Splits* illustration provided; prepare a second wall chart with a blank banana shape on it.

Procedure

1. Divide the participants into six groups of equal number. Assign each group one of the following roles: Pickers/Growers; Retailers; Wholesalers; Importing Company; Shipping Company; Packaging Company.

2. Distribute pencils and paper to each group. Give the pickers each a banana and inform everybody that a banana costs ten cents.

3. Post the chart of a blank banana marked "ten cents" on the wall and ask each group to decide what cut each role should have of the final banana price. This should be based on the amount of labor and other costs each group feels it must meet.

4. After five minutes, get each group to present its case. Write the amounts on the blank banana. If the total comes to over ten cents get them to negotiate among themselves until it comes back to ten cents.

5. Display the chart depicting the actual price breakdown. Discuss the following: How do the two sets of divisions compare? How does each role group feel about the price breakdown? What would be the fairest division of the price? How could the pickers/growers get a better cut?

6. Conclude the activity with each group taking its share from the pickers'/growers' bananas.

Source: *Banana Splits* is adapted from *Make a World of Difference* by Office on Global Education, (Baltimore: Office on Global Education, Church World Service, 1989) and used with permission.

BANANA SPLITS

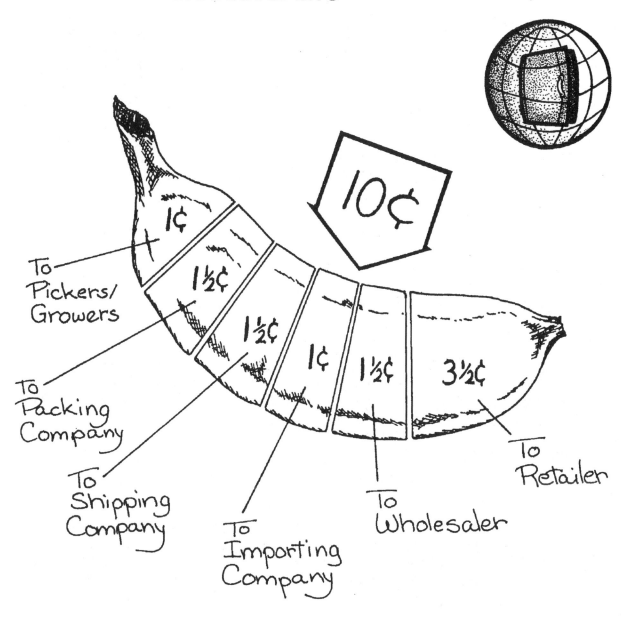

To Pickers/ Growers — 1¢

To Packing Company — 1½¢

To Shipping Company — 1½¢

To Importing Company — 1¢

To Wholesaler — 1½¢

To Retailer — 3½¢

10¢

*"We consume arms, we consume useless products, we consume everything in sight.
And we end up by consuming human beings themselves."*

Adolfo Perez Esquivel
1980 Nobel Peace Prize
Christ in a Poncho

I-6 *TAKING A STAND ON THE CAUSES OF HUNGER*

Description of Activity:

Creating a living continuum around the causes of world hunger.

Objective:

To explore individual and group assumptions about the causes of hunger in the developed and developing countries of the world.

Time:

15 minutes.

Materials:

Masking tape, *Hunger Cause Statements*.

Prior to the Activity:

Move the furniture from a section of the room in which you're be meeting. On the empty floor, put a line of masking tape that is long enough for all group members to stand behind, shoulder to shoulder. Using masking tape, mark one end of the line TA; mark the opposite end TD. Have a copy of the *Hunger Cause Statements* available for the reader.

Procedure

1. Introduce the topic. Invite the group to take a stand on the causes of world hunger by forming a human "continuum."

2. Share simple directions for the exercise. The line in front of them is a continuum — a line graph that represents their level of agreement with the statements that will be read about the causes of world hunger. To place oneself near the TA end symbolizes Total Agreement with the statements that will be read. To stand near the TD end indicates Total Disagreement. All the points in between represent varying degrees of support or dissent.

3. Explain that you'll be reading a list of eight possible causes of hunger in the developing countries of our world. After they have heard each statement, they should take a minute to consider their level of agreement or disagreement with the statement and why they think that way. When they're clear on what and why they think, they should move silently to the point on the continuum that best represents their thoughts.

4. When everyone is settled, ask one person close to each end of the continuum to share the reason for his or her stance on the continuum. Ask everyone to prepare for the next question by returning to the neutral zone in front of the continuum.

5. When the exercise is finished, discuss the feelings and learnings connected with the exercise. See if there is any group consensus around the causes of hunger in the nations of our world.

HUNGER CAUSE STATEMENTS

1. People are hungry because poor nations refuse to cut their birthrate. Lowered birthrates would guarantee adequate food for all.

2. People are hungry because food isn't shared equitably. Wealthy nations use too much of the world's resources.

3. People are hungry because governments only listen to people with power...and the hungry are powerless.

4. People are hungry because they can't find work.

5. Poor farming methods in Southeast Asia make hunger inevitable. If they used our farming methods, there would be plenty of food for all.

6. People are hungry because they're lazy. With a bit of hard work they could erase their poverty and hunger.

7. People in developing countries are hungry because richer nations aren't generous in sharing their resources.

8. The U.S. is particularly generous in sharing its resources with the poor people of the world. If every nation matched our level of giving, hunger and poverty would be wiped out in no time.

ⅠI-7 MYTHS ABOUT FOOD

Description of Activity:

True/False questionnaire on food myths.

Objective:

To explore popular myths and misconceptions about food production and consumption.

Time:

15 minutes.

Materials:

Myths About Food worksheet, pens/pencils.

Prior to the Activity:

Gather materials, duplicate *Myths About Food* worksheets for distribution to group members.

Procedure

1. Introduce the topic. Explain that there are many myths and misconceptions that surround the issue of food production and availability — and that accepting these myths can keep us from responding adequately to the problems of world poverty and hunger.

2. Distribute the *Myths* worksheet, asking group members to fill it out individually (or in pairs).

3. When the worksheets are completed, invite individuals to share their responses to each question, noting why they responded as they did. Share the statements listed on the answer sheet, asking for group suggestions about why and how we might respond differently to the issues of hunger and poverty once the myths have been debunked.

Source: *Myths About Food* questionnaire and answer sheet are taken from *Teaching Development Issues, Section 3 — Food* by David Cook and Cathy Nash (Manchester, England: Development Education Project, 1986) and used with permission.

MYTHS ABOUT FOOD

A Questionnaire

Directions: After each statement circle either

True (T), False (F), or Not Sure (N)

1) The world produces enough food to feed all the people well.   T   F   N

2) The areas of the world which suffer from food shortages are those areas which have a high population density.   T   F   N

3) Modern Western farms produce higher yields per acre than traditional Southeast Asian farming methods.   T   F   N

4) Cereal crops (e.g., wheat, corn, barley) are a very important source of food, yet 50% of the world's cereal production ends up as food for livestock.   T   F   N

5) Farmers in poor countries cannot afford to buy enough fertilizers and pesticides to enable them to produce more food.   T   F   N

6) The United States burnt or dumped into the ocean eight million tons of grain in 1981.   T   F   N

7) Many of the countries which cannot feed their people export millions of tons of cash crops, for example, tea, pineapple, peanuts, cotton.   T   F   N

8) In much of South America the farmers own their own land and are able to sell their crops to provide a good living for their families.   T   F   N

MYTHS ABOUT FOOD
An Answer Sheet

1) TRUE Enough grain alone is grown to provide each person in the world with two pounds every day. This will provide 3000 calories.

2) FALSE Areas of the world which have a high population density include Europe and parts of North America which are able to feed their people by producing manufactured goods to sell or exchange. The areas suffering from most frequent food shortages are those with relatively low densities, e.g., Sahel.

3) FALSE The highest grain yields per acre have been achieved in the delta areas of Southeast Asia where three crops of rice intensively farmed may be harvested in one year.

4) TRUE In the rich North, the demand for meat in our diets is increasing rapidly. Each American on average eats 120 pounds of beef a year. Grain is feed to beef cattle, pigs, and chickens. To produce one pound of beef, five pounds of grain must be fed to the animal.

5) TRUE Fertilizers are often made from oil and are thus expensive to buy and are beyond the pocket of the small farmer. Eighty-five percent of the world's fertilizer is used by Western Europe and North America.

6) TRUE The grain was dumped in the ocean to prevent the price paid for wheat from falling too low on the world market when there was a huge surplus. It was considered too expensive to transport the grain to countries suffering temporary shortages.

7) TRUE Mali in West Africa used to grow 60,000 tons of food. Now it only produces 15,000 tons because a large proportion of the land is used to grow cotton and peanuts which are then exported. In the West Indies, 50% of the land is used to grow coffee, bananas, and sugar while eight out of ten children are underfed. During the 1971 drought, the Sahel countries (on the edge of the Sahara desert) exported 15 million kilos of vegetables, mainly to Europe. In 1983/1984, the same area had record crops of cotton! Multinational companies control much of the best land and they grow crops for export.

8) FALSE In El Salvador, 2% of the population owns 60% of the land. This land is then rented out to poor farmers who may have to give up half of the crops they grow as rent and who have no rights to the land.

I-8 *A WORLD OF ONE HUNDRED*

Description of Activity:

Creating a symbolic representation of the world as we perceive it.

Objectives:

To judge how well our perception of the world's population matches reality; to realize how small a percentage of the world's people live in comfort or luxury.

Time:

20 minutes.

Materials:

A World of One Hundred worksheets, colored pencils/markers/crayons.

Prior to the Activity:

Gather materials, duplicate *A World of One Hundred* worksheets for distribution to group members.

Procedure

1. Introduce the topic. Divide the group into teams of 4-6 members, giving a single *World* worksheet to each team.

2. Share simple directions for the exercise. The 100 figures on the sheet in front of them represent the 5.5 billion people of the world; each individual figure represents about 55 million people. You will read off eight different categories for the world's people. After discussing the category among themselves they should circle the appropriate proportion/percentage of the world's people included in that category, differentiating between the different categories by marker color or side notation.

3. When the teams have finished their task, share the correct answers with them. Ask for their reactions to the exercise. How accurate was each team's perception of the world? Why were their perceptions of the world on or off target? Did any particular figure surprise them? Why? What thoughts or feelings might flow from this new perception of the world?

CATEGORY LISTING AND ANSWER SHEET

1. Standard of living. How many of the 100 would be numbered among the poor? How many would be considered rich? (poor 67; rich 33)

2. Race. How many of the 100 are white? How many are people of color? (white 32; people of color 68)

3. Religion. How many of the 100 are Christians? Hindus? Buddhists? Moslems? Other? No Religion? (Christians 29; Hindus 13; Buddhists 12; Moslems 14; Other 14; No Religion 18)

4. Location. How many of the 100 live in Asia? How many live in North America? (Asia 58; North America 8)

5. Food. How many of the 100 would have an adequate diet? How many would be suffering from malnutrition? How many would be starving? (adequate 62; malnutrition 25; starving 13)

6. Earnings. How many of the 100 earn less than $1000 per year? (85)

7. Age. How many of the 100 are under 15 years of age? How many over? (under 37; over 63)

8. Water. How many of the 100 have safe drinking water? How many don't? (safe water 75; unsafe water 25)

A WORLD OF ONE HUNDRED

* Each figure represents approximately 55 million people

INVOLVEMENT ACTIVITIES ABOUT POVERTY AND HUNGER

I-9 SURVIVING ON MINIMUM WAGE

Description of Activity:

Developing a monthly budget for someone working a minimum wage job.

Objective:

To help participants realize the challenges and frustrations faced by those living on fixed and inadequate incomes.

Time:

45 minutes.

Materials:

Newsprint, markers, real estate rental sections from local newspapers, *Month to Month on Minimum Wage* worksheet, pens/pencils.

Prior to the Activity:

Gather materials, duplicate *Wage* worksheet for distribution to individuals.

Procedure

1. Introduce the topic. Ask the group to identify the present minimum wage in your state. Unless the state-mandated scale is appreciably higher in your area, work with the federal figure of $4.25 per hour for the purposes of this activity.

2. Ask individuals to imagine that they're single 20-25 year-olds with a high school education. They live in your area and work at a minimum wage job. They maintain regular ties with family members, but have to get by financially on what they earn without outside help. At the $4.25 minimum wage they bring home $141 per week — $170 for 40 hours work, less federal taxes ($16) and FICA ($13). This gives them an average monthly budget of $611 to take care of all their needs. (NOTE: State and local income taxes would reduce this figure further.)

3. Divide the group into teams of 3-4, asking each team to come up with a name for the single, wage earner with whom it will be working. Using the *Wage* worksheet and rental listings, ask each team to develop a monthly budget for its individual.

4. Have each team share its budget, mentioning briefly the struggles it had in the process. Talk through some of the feelings and issues faced by team members as they struggled to survive on minimum wage.

MONTH TO MONTH ON MINIMUM WAGE

EXPENSE CATEGORY	MONTHLY ALLOTMENT
Rent...	
Heat...	
Electricity & Water	
Food	
Phone	
Education	
Transportation	
Auto (purchase & repairs; maintenance; fuel; insurance	
Public transportation...	
Clothing	
Purchase; laundry; cleaning...	
Church/Charitable gifts..	
Medical/Dental	
Insurance	
Renters; health; life...	
Savings...	
Vacation; education; major purchases	
Entertainment	
Eating out; having friends in; concerts/movies; records/tapes/books	
TOTAL EXPENDITURES	**$611**

Description of Activity:

A guided imagery experience in absolute poverty.

Objective:

To help people relate to the impact of absolute poverty on the living conditions of the world's poor.

Time:

15 minutes.

Materials:

Living in Absolute Poverty meditation; tape player; soft/instrumental music.

Prior to the Activity:

Gather materials; if possible, conduct this activity in an area where comfortable seating and dim lighting are possible.

Procedure

1. Introduce the topic. Absolute poverty is a term used to describe those who survive on 50 cents or less per day — a situation that is lived reality for more than 800 million people in our world. It is a situation that's hard for us to even comprehend. A guided imagery experience provides an opportunity to open ourselves, in a small way, to what absolute poverty means for people.

2. Prepare the group for the guided imagery experience. Dim the room's lights (if possible), play soft background music, and ask them to make themselves as physically comfortable as possible and to close their eyes. Invite the group to take slow, deep breaths, to shut out outside sensations and thoughts.

3. Slowly, lead them in the *Absolute Poverty* meditation.

4. When the meditation is finished, ask the group to remain silent for a minute or two, getting in touch with the thoughts and feelings they had during the meditation. How would they feel if they were caught in absolute poverty? How might their feelings differ from those currently living in such poverty? Why?

LIVING IN ABSOLUTE POVERTY

A Meditation

Life on 50 cents or less a day...that's a way of life for more than 800 million people in our world. A group of people almost three times the size of the entire U.S. population. Men and women. Elderly and children. People of all colors, creeds, and countries.

As hard as it is to imagine, let's try. Walk, in your mind, through the rooms of your home. Look at the furniture and appliances; check out closets and cabinet drawers. Pick out your favorite room and favorite things. Favorite clothes and favorite foods.

Now let's try to imagine what your home would be like if you were trying to survive on just 50 cents a day. First, empty the house of its furnishings. Keep just a simple table and chair...mattress and blanket...a few unmatched dishes and plates...an old cooking pot...a couple of knives, forks, and spoons.

Next, take away the closets and drawers of clothing. Keep a set of clothes to work in and, if you're lucky, another set for dress. On your feet you've got inexpensive sandals or perhaps you go barefoot. Sneakers and shoes are expensive and treated with care if and when you can afford them.

Empty the refrigerator and kitchen cupboards of their food. Keep a few pounds of rice and a bag of dried beans. Maybe some simple spices and a small jar of cooking oil. Matches and a small pile of charcoal.

The change in your pocket is what you have to survive on for the next few days. An empty glass jar or tightly rolled bandana holds your life savings — four or five dollars saved with great difficulty for emergencies.

Shut off the water and electricity. Remove sinks and toilets, light fixtures and electrical outlets. Leave your home and move into a toolshed or hastily constructed lean-to, built of scavenged wood and cardboard, held together with a few nails and pieces of wire or twine. Crowd the area with other "homes" like yours...you're now part of shanty town or slum area peopled by folks like you — down on their luck, but somehow still hopeful for change.

Decorate the walls of your home with pictures cut from calendars or magazines. Then discard all magazines and books since you're now illiterate and unable to afford the few dollars needed for school registration, books, and supplies. Move the nearest clinic or hospital miles away and put a nurse's aide in charge instead of a doctor.

Give your family three rented acres to farm. On it you can raise $300 in cash crops. One-third of that will go to the landlord and another 30 or 40 dollars to the local money lender against what you borrowed for tools or seeds, emergency food or medicine.

Add unnecessary illness and disease, and subtract 25 or 30 years from your lifespan. That's just a taste of what life is like when you live in absolute poverty.

EXPLORATION ACTIVITIES ABOUT POVERTY AND HUNGER

A s people move into *Exploration*, the second step of the Pastoral Circle, they begin to ask *how* and *why* injustice exists. *Exploration* helps us understand the elements that give birth to or sustain poverty, hunger, and homelessness in our local community or throughout the world. It explores the assumptions that allow injustice to go unchecked and the social structures that too often work against social change, consciously or not.

CONDUCTING AN EXPLORATION ACTIVITY

The *Exploration* activities included in this chapter help young people to learn more about the *how's* and *why's* of the issues they claimed as their own through *Involvement*. Check the notes in the previous section on **Preparing for** and **Conducting an Involvement Activity**. The process suggestions made there apply equally well to **Preparing for** and **Conducting an Exploration Activity**, and hence will not be repeated here. Given the nature of *Exploration* however, debriefing will be substantially different and deserves special mention here.

Discussing/Debriefing an Exploration Activity: Prior to the discussion period that is built into, or flows from the *Exploration* activity, tell the group how long the discussion will last, what the questions/issues will be, and the kind of response you are looking for. Urge all group members to contribute actively to the discussion. Encourage them to share what they have learned about:

1. *History*. How long has the problem of hunger, poverty, or homelessness been with us? How has it changed through the years? Does anyone benefit from the present situation? Who suffers?

2. *Economics*. What influence does economics have on this issue? Who controls the resources (natural and human resources, manufactured goods, and money) involved? Who benefits economically from this situation? Who suffers?

3. *Politics*. What influence does politics have on this issue? Who has the critical decision-making power in this situation? Who benefits? Who suffers?

4. *Culture and Values*. What values (e.g., patriotism, independence, inclusion, human dignity, acceptance of cultural differences) are at work or absent in this situation? Who benefits from these values? Who suffers?

5. *Connections*. Are there any links between the economic, political, and cultural structures? Does money have any influence on how political decisions are made? Do any existing cultural values or beliefs work against change in this situation?

The answers to these questions help young people to identify the specific problems that need to be addressed and the strengths on which social change can build.

The *Exploration* activities are briefly described below. Choose an activity that fits well with the topic you're exploring and your earlier approach to *Involvement*, and continue your journey around the Pastoral Circle.

AN OVERVIEW OF EXPLORATION ACTIVITIES

E-1 Down and Out in the USA *

Focus: Investigating the causes of domestic poverty and homelessness
Methods: Video presentation; discussion

E-2 Giving the Homeless a Human Face **

Focus: Exploring the causes of domestic homelessness and its impact on the lives of individuals and families
Methods: Resource reading; creating written portraits of the homeless; discussion

E-3 The Mouse's Tale *

Focus: Discovering the causes of poverty in developing countries; exploring the linkage between poverty and food production and pricing
Methods: Video presentation; discussion

E-4 The Poverty Around Me: City and State

Focus: Investigating the causes of domestic poverty
Methods: Developing a definition of poverty; panel presentation; discussion

E-5 Home from the Journey

Focus: Exploring global economic interdependence and the economic and social costs of shifting labor patterns for workers
Methods: Video or speaker presentation; discussion

E-6 Enjoying the World's Resources by the Slice

Focus: Contrasting the use of the world's resources by developed and developing countries; exploring the implications for the world's poor
Methods: Slicing a pizza, discussion

E-7 Preparing and Sharing a Global Quiz

Focus: Investigating the causes and consequences of global poverty and hunger
Methods: Group development of true/false or multiple choice quizzes on poverty and hunger; discussion

E-8 Anything-But-Trivial Pursuit **

Focus: Exploring the causes and consequences of domestic and/or global poverty
Methods: Creation of a board game based on the issues of domestic and/or global poverty; discussion

E-9 Analyzing a News Story: Reading Between the Lines

Focus: Providing the skills needed to critique media reports of justice issues
Methods: Analysis of newspaper stories and reports; discussion

---

* These activities should prove particularly effective with *younger* adolescents.

** These activities should prove particularly effective with *older* adolescents.

E-1 *DOWN AND OUT IN THE USA*

Description of Activity:

Video presentation followed by an exploration of the causes of poverty and homelessness in the United States.

Objective:

To investigate the causes of domestic poverty and homelessness.

Time:

45-90 minutes.

Materials:

Video player and monitor, *Down and Out in America* video, newsprint, markers.

Prior to the Activity:

Rent or purchase video, preview video, gather materials.

Procedure

1. Introduce the topic of homelessness and/or poverty, referencing the earlier Involvement activity.

2. Introduce the video *Down and Out in America* — a 57- minute, color video which explores the issues of poverty and homelessness in urban and rural America. The film, narrated and directed by Lee Grant, won an Academy Award in 1986 as Best Documentary.

3. View the video. If time makes it difficult to view the entire video in one sitting, the interview format of the video makes it possible to excerpt sections of the video or to view it in segments without losing the message or impact of the film.

4. Discuss the video. Brainstorm a list of the causes of homelessness and poverty mentioned in the film, writing them on newsprint for all to see. When the brainstorming is complete, try to group similar causes together under general headings, for example, urban, rural, shared; political, economic, disaster, etc. Once people become poor or homeless, what hinders them from changing their situation? How was that point shown in the film? What chance do you think the different individuals in the film have of moving out of their poverty? Could you imagine yourself or your family falling into poverty? Why or why not? In summary: What seem to be the two or three most powerful causes of poverty in the U.S.? What are the two or three most powerful factors that keep people from moving out of poverty or homelessness?

Description of Activity:

Creating written portraits of the homeless.

Objective:

To explore the causes of homelessness in the United States and understand its impact on the lives of the individuals and families involved.

Time:

40 minutes.

Materials:

Newsprint, markers, *The Causes of Modern Homelessness* reading, related newspaper/magazine articles on homelessness, paper, pens/pencils.

Prior to the Activity:

Collect newspaper/magazine stories and articles on homelessness, gather materials, duplicate *Modern Homelessness* for distribution to individuals.

Procedure

1. Introduce the topic, referencing the earlier *Involvement* activity. Distribute copies of *The Causes of Modern Homelessness* for individual reading. Ask group members to be attentive in their reading to the causes of homelessness and the implications of homelessness on the lives of the poor, that is, how people's lives are different because they are homeless.

2. When the group has finished reading, list the four causes of homelessness highlighted in the reading (Employment; Housing; Deinstitutionalization; Cutbacks in Federal Assistance) and ask the group to brainstorm the implications of each for the lives of the homeless; for example, how the lack of a well paying job impacts a person's finances, health, self-image, chances for education, or job advancement.

3. Dividing the group into teams of 3-4, ask each group to create a written portrait of a "typical" homeless person. The opening sentence for all the essays should read "My name is _____, I'm ____ years old, single/marrried/divorced/widowed, and I'm homeless." The written portrait should continue to be written in the first person. Ask that they include short, personal histories of their homeless persons, noting what life was like before homelessness, what caused or contributed to their homelessness, and how they're presently surviving homelessness. Have each team also address the implications of homelessness, short-term and long-term, on the life of its homeless individual. Magazine and newspaper stories collected prior to the session can be used as reference materials by team members in creating their written portraits of the homeless.

4. Share the stories. Ask how real the people and stories are. Discuss the emotions and reflections raised through the writing exercise.

Source: Excerpted from Mark Grinker's "The Causes of Modern Homelessness," *Food Monitor*, Winter 1988, pp. 34-37.

We have come to accept the term "homelessness" as a new addition to the English language, a term that, one can image, might someday be described in Webster's as having "come into common usageine during the latter part of the twentieth century".... We have chosen this name because it makes use of the one characteristic common to all of these individuals. But by doing so we suggest that these people are the same, facing identical problems. And it is this suggestion that is at odds with the truth of who the homeless are and how they came to be on the streets.

If we look beyond the term "homelessness," we find a quite diverse group of people and problems:

• An average of 22% of homeless individuals are employed either full- or part-time.

• One-third of the homeless are families with children.

• The city with the highest rate of growth in its homeless population in 1987 (44%) was Kansas City, Missouri, not New York nor Chicago.

• Studies show an explosion in homelessness in the most rural of areas.

• Although we have long associated homelessness, to an excessive degree, with mental disability, current statistics indicate that only approximately 30% of the homeless fall into this group.

In understanding that the homeless are actually a diverse collection of individuals who have difficulty competing for the basic requirements of life for a variety of reasons, we can begin to address specific problems. A variety of recent studies has suggested that there are four primary causes of homelessness: (1) rising rates of unemployment and underemployment, particularly among the young and minority group members; (2) a dire shortage of affordable housing; (3) poorly planned deinstitutionalization; and (4) restrictions and decreases in federal poverty and disability programs.

Employment: From 1960 to 1980, the country saw a 20% decrease in manufacturing jobs, which were generally middle-income positions with at least adequate benefits, such as health insurance and pensions. New jobs created during this period, and those currently being created, primarily have consisted of low-paid, often minimum-wage, retail, service, and assembly jobs without the same array of employment benefits.

With divorce rates higher in the last 20 years than at any previous time, women have become the head of household in millions of families. Yet, as the average salary for a woman in the United States is only 64.3% of that of men, and since more than half of the households in this country require two wage earners to make ends meet, single-parent, female-headed households have become a cliché of modern poverty.

The low minimum wage, the lower average salary for women as compared to men, and the dearth of adequate employment opportunities for unskilled workers and displaced skilled workers, all have contributed to the shocking phenomenon of the employed homeless. As our consciences accept that a person can work a 40-hour week and not afford a place to live, we must conclude that something is wrong with the economy.

Housing: The combined effects of unemployment and underemployment, deinstitutionalization, and cutbacks in federal assistance programs have created a greater need for "housing of last resort," specifically "single room occupancy" hotels, rooming houses, and the like. But just as the need for this housing was reaching a peak in the early 1980s, urban renewal, abandonment, and gentrification had combined to produce the lowest level of available "last resort" housing in memory. From 1970 to 1982, 1,160,000 single-room units were lost, nearly half of the total nationwide.

Closer to the top of the market, we have been confronted with a growing polarization between the wages of those on the highest rungs of the economic ladder, who control a rapidly growing share of the nation's wealth, and those at the bottom of that ladder, who ended up with the new, lower-paying jobs in the economic transformation that characterized the 1970s. The need to house a new class of gentry produced the economic incentive for displacement of existing low-income, private-sector housing, while creating increased competition and higher prices for a decreasing number of lower-priced housing units.

Fewer new entrants into the housing market have been able to afford to buy their first home, due to record real estate prices, and were left to seek rental units. The competition for these units increased prices at the top of the rental market, and many young people sought rental housing in the middle of the market, effectively increasing the number of people seeking the short supply of even lower rent units. Contrary to the "laws" of supply and demand, this new demand for moderate and low-rent housing did not result in an increase of supply.

Deinstitutionalization: Nearly 30% of the homeless population is mentally disabled. The wave of deinstitutionalization, which saw the in-patient populations of psychiatric institutions fall from 505,000 in 1963 to 138,000 in 1980, is a component of this problem.

At first, the deinstitutionalized patient often sought housing in single-room occupancy hotels, adult homes, or other similar facilities. However, the combined forces of eviction or other displacement of these individuals (often due to their inability to manage finances or other basic aspects of life) and the steady disappearance of "last resort" housing, produced a population without homes and without access to a living situation that compensated for their disabilities.

Cutbacks in Federal Assistance: Just as the conditions for a wide-spread crisis of homelessness were reaching their peak in 1980, the nation elected a new President committed to reducing government spending on social programs. The looming explosion in homelessness created by the failure of the American economic and social systems to create opportunity for all citizens was to be mixed with a governing philosophy that essentially required the very same free-market capitalism to make up for its own shortcomings. In reality, the cutbacks in disability, Aid to Families with Dependent Children (AFDC), and Food Stamp benefits accelerated the day of reckoning.

Since 1981, AFDC eligibility and payment standards have been tightened three times, removing large numbers of families from eligibility or reducing their benefits. As AFDC payments are cut, or fail to keep pace with inflation, families often are forced to choose between food and shelter.

Exacerbating the horror of this choice is the $6.8 billion cut in the Food Stamp program, resulting in reduced benefits for 20 million people, most of whom are children, and forcing one million people out of the program entirely. The average food-stamp benefit is now 55 cents per meal.

Conclusion

Homelessness has become a stark symbol of our failure as a nation to meet even minimum standards of equity in the distribution of our resources. Decisive action at the federal level is urgently needed. While the problems are severe and the roots are deep, solutions do exist and can be implemented speedily. Both executive and legislative action must be taken now.

E-3 THE MOUSE'S TALE

Description of Activity:

Video presentation followed by discussion on global poverty and hunger.

Objectives:

To explore the causes of poverty in the developing countries of the world; understand the linkage between world poverty and issues of food production and pricing, human rights and global interdependence.

Time:

30-45 minutes.

Materials:

Video player and monitor, *The Mouse's Tale* video, newsprint, markers, paper, pens/pencils.

Prior to the Activity:

Rent or purchase video, preview video, prepare questions, gather materials.

Procedure

1. Introduce the topic of world poverty and hunger, referencing the earlier *Involvement* activity.

2. Introduce the video *The Mouse's Tale* — a 10-minute, animated video produced by Australian Catholic Relief. The video provides a short, insightful, and humorous look at some of the basic issues involved in the food crisis throughout the world that lead to starvation and extreme poverty. List on newsprint seven issues briefly explored in the video, asking the group to listen closely to what the video says about each. The seven issues are: food production, pricing and supply; education and literacy; credit for the poor; health and hygiene; community development; rights to land, jobs, income, and government aid.

3. View the video. Working in pairs, have group members jot down the causes of poverty and hunger presented by the video, and the connection between poverty and the issues listed prior to the viewing on newsprint.

4. As a large group, share reflections on the causes of poverty and the connections between global poverty and the other issues mentioned. Discuss the good approaches to aid mentioned in the video as a starting point for eradicating global poverty.

Note: A Discussion and Study Guide on *The Mouse's Tale* is available from Catholic Relief Services. See Resources page 135.

E-4 THE POVERTY AROUND ME: CITY AND STATE

Description of Activity:

Developing a common definition of poverty; speaker or panel presentation on the reality and causes of poverty in the local area (city and state).

Objective:

To explore the level and causes of poverty on the local level.

Time:

45-90 minutes.

Materials:

Paper, pens/pencils, *Poverty Definitions Sheet*.

Prior to the Activity:

Contact local church or social service agencies to arrange for speaker(s); duplicate *Definitions* for distribution to group members, gather materials.

Procedure

1. Introduce the topic of domestic/U.S. and local poverty, referencing the earlier *Involvement* activity.

2. Divide the group into teams of 3-4, assigning them the task of developing a definition of poverty appropriate to their city and state. Share definitions, noting differences and similarities. Using one of the team definitions as a base, try to establish a common group definition/description of poverty for your city and state. Distribute the *Poverty Definitions Sheet*, comparing and contrasting the definitions offered therein with your group definition.

3. Have a local advocate for the poor (social worker, counselor, or shelter director) or a small panel address the group on the issue of poverty on the local level. Issues they may wish to address include the following: What is the makeup of the poor locally? What are the causes of their poverty? How has the number of the poor changed in the past 5 to 10 years? Why? What services are available locally for the poor? What needs are left unmet by present programs or services? Why should we care about the poor? What could we do, if we wanted, to change the situation of the poor? The presentation, time permitting, should be followed by a general question/answer session.

Source: Definitions adapted from *Cry of the Poor* by Tom Larkin and Pauline McAndrew (Navan, Ireland: Columban Mission Education Department, 1989) and used with permission.

POVERTY DEFINITIONS SHEET

Preliminary Comments

Poverty can be looked at from many different aspects: economic poverty, political powerlessness, cultural and social rejection, and inequality.

Extreme poverty can be recognized fairly easily: if people suffer from homelessness, hunger or malnutrition, or extreme hardship, poverty obviously exists.

Inequality is not the same as poverty, but it is directly related to it and needs to be included in any discussion of poverty.

In some senses, poverty is a relative term that is defined differently in different places and at different times. Unfortunately, absolute poverty remains a constant in our world, and while definitions may change, poverty somehow seems to be always among us.

Definitions: Absolute Poverty

"Poverty so severe that people cannot meet even their basic needs for food, clothing, and shelter." (Combat Poverty, *1988*)

"More than 800 million people are in absolute poverty with no hope of breaking out of the cycle of hunger, disease and ignorance! Hundreds of millions live on 50 cents a day or less. They are hungry most of the time." (World Bank Report, *1985*)

Definitions: Relative Poverty

"Individuals, families, and groups in a population can be said to be in poverty when they lack the resources to obtain the type of diet, participate in the activities, and have the living conditions and amenities which are customary or are at least widely encouraged and approved in the society to which they belong. Their resources are so seriously below those commanded by the average individual or family that they are, in effect, excluded from ordinary living patterns, customs, and activities." (Peter Townsend, *1979*)

"If you are poor in Ireland today you are likely to be marginalised and excluded from many of the main opportunities in society and to feel powerless to change things; to have inadequate educational opportunities; to suffer from poor health and to have inadequate access to health care; to suffer unemployment or to be in and out of low paid jobs; and to have poor access to public transport." (Combat Poverty Agency Annual Report, *1987*)

E-5 *HOME FROM THE JOURNEY*

Description of Activity:

Video and/or speaker on the changes in the industrial sector which impact the poor of both developed and developing nations.

Objectives:

To explore the expanded economic interdependence of developed and developing nations throughout the world; to understand the economic and social costs of shifting labor patterns for workers, especially women, in the U.S. and abroad.

Time:

60-90 minutes.

Materials:

Video player and monitor, *The Global Assembly Line* video, newsprint, markers.

Prior to the Activity:

Rent or purchase video, preview video; contact local business, labor, or church leaders familiar with local and international assembly industry; and/or contact local residents who are themselves from, or who have worked or traveled extensively in the developing nations of Latin America or the Caribbean.

Procedure

1. Introduce the topic of global economic interdependence and its implications for workers both in the U.S. and abroad, referencing the earlier *Involvement* activity.

2. Introduce the video *The Global Assembly Line* — a 60-minute, color video produced by Educational TV and Film Center. The film features interviews with the factory workers and corporate officers of several multinational businesses.

3. View the video. Given the multiplicity of interviews in the video, segments can be selected for viewing if time is limited.

4. Discuss the video. Explore together: How has business changed over the course of the past 10-20 years? What about these changes seems good? What about these changes seems bad? How does our country benefit from these shifts? How does it suffer? How do developing countries of the world benefit? How do they suffer? What changes could, or should be made so that everybody gains most from the shift to an increasingly international business economy? What would these changes demand or look like in the factories pictured in the video? How would these changes impact the lives of the workers featured in the film? What would the changes cost? Who would bear the cost? Is the cost worth it?

— And/Or —

5. Introduce the speaker(s) who will be addressing the group, noting the particular focus of the issues. If you are not introducing the session with the video, have the speakers highlight the growing internationalization of our economy and its impact on workers and consumers. After a brief presentation, open the discussion up to the large group. Keep discussion focused on both the causes and consequences of the change for the people of the US and the developing countries of our world, both workers and consumers.

Source: *Home from the Journey* adapted from *Make a World of Difference* by Global Education Office, CWS (Baltimore: Friendship Press, 1989) and used with permission.

E-6 ENJOYING THE WORLD'S RESOURCES BY THE SLICE

Description of Activity:

A comparison of the world's population and energy consumption by continent.

Objectives:

To illustrate graphically the great discrepancy in the use of world resources between developed and developing nations; to explore the implications of the discrepancy for the poor of the world.

Time:

20 minutes.

Materials:

Slices of the World chart, two large cheese pizzas (loaded with everything but anchovies), napkins, sharp knife; newsprint, markers, paper, pens/pencils.

Prior to the Activity:

Order pizzas for delivery at start of group session*; gather materials.

Procedure

1. Introduce the topic of equitable distribution of the world's resources. Note that two of the world's most prized resources, fully-loaded pizzas are on the table in front of them. Offer them a quick look at the pizzas; invite them, from where they are sitting to breathe in its wonderful aroma. Tell them that henceforth in this gathering, they represent the entire population of the planet, and that the pizzas, henceforth, aren't really food, but pie graphs contrasting the world's population and energy use by region.

2. Working in teams of 4-6, have the group quickly draw two pie graphs. The first should represent the breakdown of the world into population groups. The second should take these same areas and illustrate the percentage of the world's energy consumed by each region. The areas to be included are: Asia, Latin America, North America, Russia, Europe, and Africa.

3. Post and compare pie graphs. (Quickly, please. The pizzas are getting cool.)

4. Ask everyone to gather round as you cut the initial pizza, representing the population breakdown by region. Cut the second pizza according to energy consumption by region. Note that if the pizza toppings were distributed in keeping with the actual use of the world's resources, most would be piled high on the North America, Europe, and Russia population slices. Ask the group how they think the pie should be cut. Make the appropriate additional cuts. Enjoy eating the special "graphics."

*SPECIAL NOTE: When ordering pizzas, make a special request that they not be cut before delivery.

SLICES OF THE WORLD

Pizza Pie Illustration of Population and Energy Consumption

POPULATION

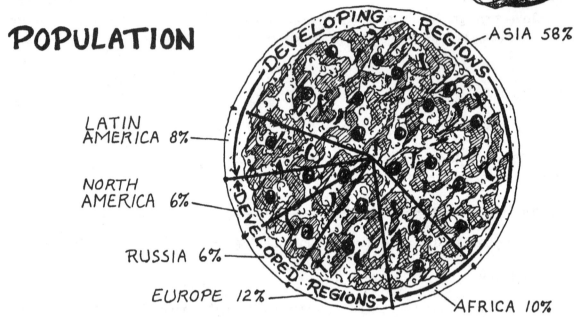

ASIA 58%

LATIN AMERICA 8%

NORTH AMERICA 6%

RUSSIA 6%

EUROPE 12%

AFRICA 10%

DEVELOPING REGIONS

DEVELOPED REGIONS

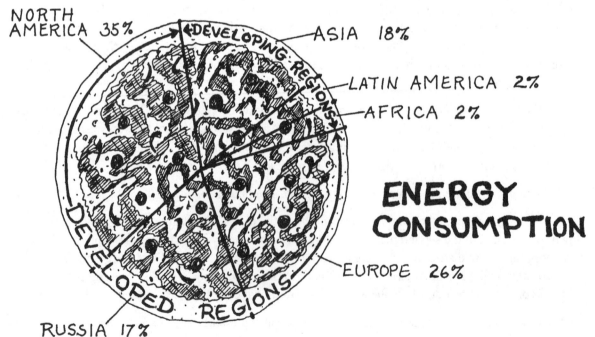

NORTH AMERICA 35%

ASIA 18%

LATIN AMERICA 2%

AFRICA 2%

DEVELOPING REGIONS

DEVELOPED REGIONS

ENERGY CONSUMPTION

EUROPE 26%

RUSSIA 17%

E-7 PREPARING AND SHARING A GLOBAL QUIZ

Description of Activity:

Small group creation of a true/false, multiple choice, or essay quiz around the issues of global poverty and hunger.

Objective:

To investigate the causes and consequences of global poverty and hunger.

Time:

60-90 minutes.

Materials:

Paper, pens/pencils, resource materials on the causes and consequences of global poverty and hunger.

Prior to the Activity:

Gather materials.

Procedure

1. Introduce the topic referencing the earlier *Involvement* activity.

2. Divide the group into teams of 4-6, assigning them the task of developing a true/false, multiple choice, or essay quiz on the causes and consequences of global poverty and hunger.

3. Emphasize that the point of the exercise isn't to unearth trivia that others won't be able to answer, but to use the quiz-making strategy as a means of helping people become more aware of the major causes and consequences of global poverty and/or hunger. The quiz sheets should be accompanied by answer sheets that reference the sources of their material or provide simple background material. Reference materials should be available for their use. Suggested resources are included in the Resource section of this book. Three key resources you may want to use are: *The Big Picture* and *Global Realities Fact Sheet* produced by Catholic Relief Services and *Global Poverty and Personal Responsibility* by Elizabeth Morgan.

4. When the teams have completed their assignments, take turns "quizzing" one another, possibly over several sessions with input and discussion in-between. Discuss the group's learnings while preparing and sharing their quizzes. Ask the group to be particularly attentive to any connections between the various expressions of poverty, for example, if lack of full-time employment is pointed out as a primary cause of hunger, ask how this same factor impacts a family's ability to provide adequate health care or education for its members.

Description of Activity:

Creation of a board game, modelled on Trivial Pursuit™, but using game pieces and cards which speak to issues of domestic and/or global poverty.

Objective:

To explore the causes and consequences of domestic and/or global poverty.

Time:

2-3 hours.

Materials:

Posterboard, index cards, color markers/pens/pencils, dice, stop watch or timer, writings and statistics on the causes and consequences of domestic and/or global poverty.

Prior to the Activity:

Collect resource writings/statistics, gather program materials.

Procedure

1. Introduce the topic of global or domestic poverty referencing the earlier *Involvement* activity. Explain the activity and its purpose. As emphasized in the title of this activity, this game is not about trivia, but about the actual causes and real-life consequences of poverty.

2. Divide the group into six equal teams. Assign each team one of the following (or similar) topics: Peoples and Places of the World; A Typical Day in the USA; Hunger Myths and Facts; What Money Can Buy; Women and Children in the Global Village; Health and Education; Causes and Consequences, Signs of Hope. Using the reference materials gathered (or resourcing the topic between group meetings), ask each team to create 20 game cards around its issue/concern. The topic area and questions should be printed on the front of the index card and the answer on the back. An option for more difficult questions would be to have game participants select their response from three or four possible choices listed beneath the question on the front of the game card.

3. Have volunteers create game pieces and a gameboard that reflect the uniqueness of this Anything-But-Trivial activity.

4. When the teams have finished their assigned task, discuss and decide together possible rules for play. Working with the same teams, play a game of Anything-But-Trivial Pursuit. Emphasize that more important than winning the game is understanding how the pieces of poverty fit together and how we can act to change the game so that everyone in the world gets a better chance to survive and thrive in the world.

E-9 *ANALYZING A NEWS STORY: READING BETWEEN THE LINES*

Description:

Analysis of newspaper stories and reports on domestic and global poverty, hunger, and homelessness.

Objective:

To provide young people with the skills needed to critique the news media and uncover possible bias in reporting of justice issues.

Time:

40 minutes.

Materials:

Paper, pens/pencils, news articles from several different newspapers or magazines on the issue being studied, *How to Analyze a News Story* sheets.

Prior to the Activity:

Gather materials, duplicate *How to Analyze* sheets for distribution to group members.

Procedure

1. Introduce the topic. Ask the group to describe/define the word "objectivity" and give examples of what it would mean in reporting on issues of social justice.

2. Distribute the *How to Analyze* sheets, asking group members to read through the sheets individually. Respond to any questions they group have.

3. Divide the group into teams of 3-4. Give two or three of the previously selected news articles to each group, asking them to analyze the articles, using the eight guidelines outlined in the *How to Analyze* resource sheets. Ask each group to prepare a brief report on their analysis.

4. Share team findings with the large group. Discuss together: How "objective" do the stories appear to be? In the facts shared? In the values upheld? Is objectivity always a good thing? Why or why not? Is there much difference in reporting style or article content from one news source to another? Why or why not? What is the responsibility of reporters in constructing their stories? What is the responsibility of the news "consumers" in reading what's written for them? What suggestions would they make to help young people be better consumers of the information and values shared by the news media?

Source: Guidelines sheets taken from "How to Analyze a News Story," *Media and Values*, Spring 1990, and used with permission.

HOW TO ANALYZE A NEWS STORY

Eight Guidelines for Reading between the Lines

1. Compare headlines and story content. Headlines are probably the most important aspect of news stories. Most people "shop" headlines to determine which articles to read. After reading an article, propose alternative headlines that emphasize different facts.

• *How accurately does the actual headline encapsulate the article? Does the headline slant one's reading of the article?*

2. Identify politically-charged labels, adjectives, and verbs. Word choices can help identify reporters' biases. Have your family or group read an article and list words that seem politically charged. For example:

Are those who support abortion rights called "abortion activists" or "pro-choice activists?" What connotation does the word "activist" imply? Why?

3. Question the hidden agenda of suspicious sources. Sometimes reporters need to speak with sources "off the record." Often, however, sources use their anonymity to further their own agendas.

• *When a reporter cites "top U.S. officials," "company informants," or other anonymous sources, whose position is left out? What ulterior motive might a source have?*

4. Consider whether the placement of ideas and sources affects story impact. Try cutting apart a newspaper article and pasting it back together in a different order.

• *Does the tenor of the article change when dissenting opinions become the lead? Whose position is stressed by the original placement of the story?*

5. Look for non-white, non-male perspectives. North American media rely heavily on white, male officials for their news.

   • *How does the news change when seen from the perspective of women or other races?*

For a class or group project, have group members tally the sex and race of sources cited in a television, radio, or print report.

   • *How many are white and male? How many are females or people of color?*

6. Compare photographs and photo captions to the news stories connected with them. Manipulation of digital images is not the only way to change the meaning of a picture. As with headlines, readers "shop" a newspaper by scanning pictures and reading captions — whether or not they read the associated articles.

   •*A re photographs and their captions faithful to the articles connected with them? How does a picture or caption influence the meaning of an article?*

7. Compare news stories to common sense. Be aware of obvious misstatements of facts that defy common sense. In the aftermath of the Exxon oil spill, one article stated that much of the oil spill "is gone, most by natural action."

   • *So where did it go? Did it evaporate — or is it now mixed with billions of gallons of water?*

8. Be suspicious of polls and statistics. Polling data and statistics are notoriously deceptive.

   • *Ask "which perspective does this data seem to support?" Then try rearranging the same data so that it presents a different perspective.*

REFLECTION ACTIVITIES ABOUT POVERTY AND HUNGER

Something within us proclaims that poverty, hunger, and homelessness destroy people's dignity and just shouldn't exist. Through *Reflection*, the third step of the Pastoral Circle, we take a critical look at the religious traditions and values that challenge injustice and offer an alternative vision of how life can and should be.

CONDUCTING A REFLECTION ACTIVITY

As was the case with *Involvement* and *Exploration*, *Reflection* demands good preparation and debriefing if it is to be effective. Suggestions on **Preparing for** and **Conducting a Reflection Activity** differ little from those listed earlier in the chapters on *Involvement* and *Reflection* and will not be repeated here. Debriefing the *Reflection* activity, however, involves a unique approach and is, therefore, highlighted below.

Discussing/Debriefing a Reflection Activity: Prior to the discussion period that is built into, or flows from the *Reflection* activity, tell the group how long the discussion will last, what the questions will be, and the kind of response you are looking for. Urge all group members to contribute actively to the discussion. Encourage them to share what they have learned about:

1. *Religious Values.* What are the religious beliefs and values that seem to be at stake in the issues of poverty and hunger? What beliefs and values lead you to say, "Things shouldn't be this way!"

2. *Scripture.* How have the values you've identified been reflected in the Hebrew and Christian Scriptures? How has God's word of justice been revealed in the history of the Hebrew people? How was this issue approached by the teachers, prophets, or psalmists of the Hebrew Scriptures? What did Jesus say or do when confronted by the same or similar instances of injustice? What can be learned from the life of the early Christian community as it tried to fashion a new community around Jesus' teachings and lifestyle? What key learnings do we gain about poverty and hunger from Scripture?

3. *Church History and Tradition.* The Church's understanding of God's justice continues to grow and develop through time. In the course of its long history, has the Church community been faced before with the challenges raised by poverty and hunger? When? How did the Church respond? What principles or approaches are set forth in the Church's Social Teaching, either Vatican documents or pastoral letters developed by national bishops' conferences? Do the recent writings of the American Bishops, for example, their pastoral letters on peace, economy, racism, and international relations, offer any guidance on how we should respond today to poverty and hunger?

---

4. *The Church in Action*. Like Jesus, the Christian community speaks not just through what it says, but by how it embodies its words in action. What is the Church doing locally/nationally/internationally to respond to the short or long term problems created by poverty and hunger? Why do Christians work to relieve the problems caused by poverty, hunger, and homelessness? How do they benefit from the work they are doing?

Some topics will lend themselves better to a particular approach to *Reflection*. *Reflection* upon local poverty could easily include a visit to a nearby soup kitchen to see the Church in action; *Reflection* upon international issues, on the other hand, may rely more heavily on an examination of contemporary Church writings. The activities highlighted in this chapter offer a variety of approaches to *Reflection*. Each activity builds on the content and method shared in the previous *Involvement* and *Exploration* steps. Each challenges young people to closely examine the vision and values of Jesus and to incorporate them in the life of today's Christian community. Choose an activity that flows from your earlier *Involvement* and *Exploration* experiences and move into the *Reflection* step of the Pastoral Circle.

AN OVERVIEW OF REFLECTION ACTIVITIES

R-1 *Lazarus and the Rich Man - A Parable for Today*

Focus: Examining Jesus' teaching on wealth and its implications for today
Methods: Video presentation; discussion

R-2 *Zacchaeus: The Morning After*

Focus: Exploring the challenges embodied in Jesus' call to stewardship and simplicity
Methods: Creative writing; discussion

R-3 *But I Say to You... ***

Focus: Investigating the Christian basis for service to the poor and needy
Methods: Creative writing, contrasting popular wisdom and wisdom of Jesus; discussion

R-4 *Implications for Me and Mine*

Focus: Exploring the implications of the Church's justice teaching for individuals, for the local community, and for national/international bodies and structures
Methods: Reflection on key excerpts from Scripture and Catholic Social Teaching; discussion

R-5 *Thy Will Be Done: A Word of Witness*

Focus: Investigating the local church's response to the needs of the poor; contact with those who work directly with or speak out in advocacy for the poor
Methods: Speaker/panel presentation; discussion

R-6 *Preparing and Praying*

Focus: Reflection on key excerpts from Scripture and Catholic Social Teaching; exploring the relationship between reflection and action
Methods: Preparing a prayer experience on the issue of poverty/hunger; discussion

R-7 *Keeping the Good News New ***

Focus: Applying the principle themes of Catholic Social Teaching to contemporary issues
Methods: Developing an advertising campaign to spread the Church's Social Teaching; discussion

R-8 *Beyond Our Borders ****

Focus: Exploring the implications of economic justice for international and transnational business practices
Methods: Writing project, summarizing the international section of the economics pastoral and applying it to the situation of farm and factory workers in developing countries; discussion

R-9 *Pope for a Day*

Focus: Understanding that Catholic Social Teaching is still evolving and that the Church's response varies with different issues and settings
Methods: Creative writing, developing a papal letter to the youth of America

---

* These activities should prove particularly effective with *younger* adolescents.

** These activities should prove particularly effective with *older* adolescents.

R-1 *LAZARUS AND THE RICH MAN —*
A PARABLE FOR TODAY

Description of Activity:

Video presentation followed by discussion on the Gospel challenge to stewardship.

Objective:

To explore Jesus' teachings on wealth and examine its implications for individuals and institutions today.

Time:

40 minutes.

Materials:

Video player and monitor, *Between the Times: The Catholic Bishops and the U.S. Economy* video, newsprint, markers.

Prior to the Activity:

Rent or purchase video, preview segment of video entitled *Lazarus and the Rich Man*, prepare questions on video segment, gather materials.

Procedure

1. Introduce the topic of wealth and poverty, referencing the earlier *Involvement* and Exploration activities.

2. Introduce *Lazarus and the Rich Man* — a humorous, five-minute presentation of Jesus' story about the use and abuse of wealth (Lk 16:19-31).

3. View the video.

4. Discuss the video. What did group members most like about the video presentation of Luke's Gospel story? What did they least like? Why? In ten words or less, what was the parable of the story? Was the story addressed just to individuals, or is there a message in the story for groups and institutions as well? If there's a message in the story for institutions, what might it be?

5. Divide the group into teams of 4-6. Distribute newsprint and markers to each team. Ask them to draw a line down the center of the newsprint, labelling one side Individual and the other Institutional. Their assignment: If we took the story of Lazarus and the Rich Man to heart, what would be the implications be for us as individuals? What implications might there be for the institutions of which we are part? List five implications under each heading. When teams have finished their task, contrast and compare lists.

Description of Activity:

Composing an imaginary letter from Zacchaeus to a high school friend.

Objective:

To explore the challenges inherent in accepting Jesus' call to stewardship and simplicity.

Time:

30 minutes.

Materials:

Bibles/copies of the Zaccheus story, *Zach's Letter to a High School Friend* sheet, paper, pens/pencils.

Prior to the Activity:

Gather materials, duplicate copies of *Zach's Letter* for distribution to group members.

Procedure

1. Introduce the topics of stewardship and simplicity, referencing the earlier *Involvement* and *Exploration* activities.

2. Read together the story of Zacchaeus (Lk 19:1-10). Beforehand, ask everyone to imagine that they're Zacchaeus and that they're seeing what he saw and feeling what he felt.

3. Discuss the story. What might have led Zacchaeus to join the group waiting for Jesus' arrival? Why do you think Jesus picked Zacchaeus out of the crowd? How did Zacchaeus respond? Why? What might Zacchaeus have been thinking and feeling during this first encounter with Jesus? Why did Zacchaeus bring money into the conversation, pledging to give up half his life savings and pay back anyone he may have cheated? What do stewardship and simplicity have to do with following Jesus? What might Jesus expect of us today?

4. Ask the group to picture themselves as Zacchaeus again. But now it's the morning after his meeting and meal with Jesus. Zacchaeus, Zach for short, is trying to make sense of all that's happened to him — an amazing mix of new thoughts, feelings, and commitments. Zach tries to put down in writing what he's thinking and feeling in a letter to a friend from Jericho High. You are Zach. Write his letter, using the *Zach Letter* worksheet, sharing with your friend what's happened in your life and what you think it might mean for your future.

5. Invite individuals to read their Zach Letters. How many of the thoughts and feelings expressed belong to Zach? How many of the thoughts and feelings reflect their own?

ZACH'S LETTER
TO A HIGH SCHOOL FRIEND

DEAR

YOUR FRIEND,

ZACH

R-3 *BUT I SAY TO YOU...*

Description of Activity:

Creative writing experience contrasting "popular wisdom" with the wisdom of Jesus.

Objective:

To explore the Christian basis for service to the poor and needy.

Time:

30-45 minutes.

Materials:

Bibles, newsprint, markers, paper, pens/pencils, *But I Say To You* worksheet.

Prior to the Activity:

Gather materials, duplicate *But I Say To You* worksheet for distribution to group members.

Procedure

1. Introduce the topic of Christian response to poverty and hunger, referencing the earlier *Involvement* and *Exploration* activities.

2. Distribute *But I Say To You* worksheet. Working in pairs, have teams develop Christian responses to the "popular wisdom" statements, referring to the biblical passages cited as they see fit.

3. Share responses. Try to come up with a single, mutually acceptable Christian response to each of the "popular wisdom" statements. List these communal responses on newsprint. Discuss the implications of these statements for the issues explored earlier.

BUT I SAY TO YOU

POPULAR WISDOM SUGGESTS	THE WISDOM OF JESUS RESPONDS
1. Take good care of yourself. Watch out for number one.	2 Corinthians 8: 8-15
2. Charity begins at home.	James 2: 14-17
3. The little I can do won't make a difference.	Mark 12: 41-44
4. The one who gets the most toys wins!	Matthew 19:16-30
5. Invest for tomorrow.	Luke 12: 13-21
6. Keep to your own group; avoid those in need.	Matthew 25: 31-46

R-4 *IMPLICATIONS FOR ME AND MINE*

Description of Activity:

Reading of key excerpts from Scripture or Church Social Teaching followed by personal reflection and sharing.

Objective:

To explore the implications of the Church's justice teaching for individuals, for the local community, and for national/international bodies and structures.

Time:

30-45 minutes.

Materials:

Paper, pens/pencils, *The Scriptures Speak on Justice* or *The Church Speaks on Justice* resource sheets.

Prior to the Activity:

Gather materials, duplicate *Scriptures Speak* or *Church Speaks* sheets for distribution to group members.

Procedure

1. Introduce the topic of Christian response to poverty and hunger, referencing the earlier *Involvement* and *Exploration* activities.

2. Suggest that as Christians we need to work for justice on three different levels: the personal level (individually, as families, and with close friends); communal level (as members of neighborhoods and schools, as parishioners and workers); structural/societal level (as members of towns, states, and nations; as people who are part of, and benefit from economic, political, and social structures). Discuss the role that each of these levels plays in shaping us as people. To grow as whole people we need to be supported on all three levels. Ill treatment or injustice on any level hampers our growth as individuals and as a people.

3. Distribute the resource sheets chosen for this session. Working individually, ask members to read through the resource sheets, jotting down the implications of the Scripture or Church teachings for life on the personal, communal, and structural levels.

4. Split the group into three teams — Personal, Communal and Structural. Have each team come up with a list of six key implications of the scriptural or Church teachings for life at its level. Share and discuss as a large group.

THE SCRIPTURES SPEAK ON JUSTICE

Do not mistreat or oppress a foreigner; remember that you were foreigners in Egypt. Do not mistreat any widow or orphan. If you do, I the Lord, will answer them whey they cry out to me for help. (Ex 22: 20-24)

All riches and wealth come from you; you rule everything by your strength and power; and you are able to make anyone great and strong. (1Chr 29: 12)

Do not take revenge on anyone or continue to hate him, but love your neighbor as yourself. I am the Lord. (Lv 19: 18)

Speak up for people who cannot speak for themselves. Protect the rights of all who are helpless. Speak for them and be a righteous judge. Protect the rights of the poor and needy. (Pr 31: 8-9)

But the Lord is king forever; God has set up a judgement throne and rules the world with righteousness, judging the nations with justice. The Lord is a refuge for the oppressed, a place of safety in times of trouble. Those who know you, Lord, will trust you; you do not abandon anyone who comes to you. Sing praise to the Lord who rules in Zion! Tell every nation what God has done! God remembers those who suffer; God does not forget their cry, but punishes those who wrong them. (Ps 9: 7-12)

God will teach us what we should do; we will walk the paths God has chosen...God will settle disputes among great nations. They will hammer their swords into plows and their spears into pruning knives. Nations will never again go to war, never prepare for battle again. (Is 2: 3-4)

The kind of fasting I want is this: Remove the chains of oppression and the yoke of injustice, and let the oppressed go free. Share your food with the hungry and open your homes to the homeless poor. Give clothes to those who have nothing to wear, and do not refuse to help your own relatives. (Is 58: 6-7)

After Jesus had washed their feet, he put his outer garment back on and returned to his place at the table. "Do you understand what I have just done to you?" he asked. "You call me Teacher and Lord, and it is right that you do so, because that is what I am. I, your Lord and Teacher, have just washed your feet. I have set an example for you, so that you will do just what I have done for you. I am telling you the truth: no slave is greater than his master, and no messenger is greater than the one who sent him. Now that you know this truth, how happy you will be if you put it into practice. (Jn 13: 12-20)

If one of you wants to be great, he must be the servant of the rest; and if one of you wants to be first, he must be the slave of all. For even the Son of Man did not come to be served; he came to serve and to give his life to redeem many people. (Mk 10: 43-45)

You have heard that it was said, "An eye for an eye, and a tooth for a tooth." But now I tell you: do not take revenge on someone who wrongs you. If anyone slaps you on the right cheek, let him slap your left cheek too. And if someone takes you to court to sue you for your shirt, let him have your coat as well. And if one of the occupation troops forces you to carry his pack one mile, carry it two miles. When someone asks you for something, give it to him; when someone wants to borrow something lend it to him. You have heard that it was said, "Love your friends, hate your enemies." But now I tell you: love your enemies and pray for those who persecute you, so that you may become children of your father in heaven. (Mt 5:38-45)

All the believers continued together in close fellowship and shared their belongings with one another. They would sell their property and possessions, and distribute the money among all, according to what each needed (Ac 2: 43-45).

This is what I ask of you, only this: To act justly, to love tenderly, to walk humbly with your God. (Mi 6:8)

REFLECTION ACTIVITIES ABOUT POVERTY AND HUNGER

THE CHURCH SPEAKS ON JUSTICE

Action on behalf of justice and participation in the transformation of the world fully appear to us as a constitutive dimension of the preaching of the Gospel, or in other words, of the Church's mission for the redemption of the human race and its liberation from every oppressive situation. (*Justice in the World*, 1971 Synod of Bishops, 6)

We believe the person is sacred — the clearest reflection of God among us. Human dignity comes from God, not from nationality, race, sex, economic status, or any human accomplishment. We judge any economic situation by what it does for and to people and by how it permits all to participate in it. The economy should serve people, not the other way around. (*A Pastoral Message, Economic Justice for All*, NCCB 1986, ix)

But first we must speak of man's rights. He has the right to live. He has the right to bodily integrity and to the means necessary for the proper development of life, particularly food, clothing, shelter, medical care, rest, and finally, the necessary social services...Moreover, man has a natural right to be respected...He has a right to freedom in investigating the truth...He has the right to share in the benefits of culture, and hence to receive a good general education, and a technical or professional training consistent with the degree of educational development in his own country...In the economic sphere, it is evident that a man has the inherent right not only to be given the opportunity to work, but also to be allowed the exercise of personal initiative in the work he does. (*Peace on Earth*, Pope John XXIII, 1963, 11-27)

Economic and social policies as well as the organization of the work world should be continually evaluated in light of their impact on the strength and stability of family life. The long-range future of this nation is intimately linked with the well-being of families, for the family is the most basic form of human community. (*Economic Justice for All*, NCCB 1986, 93)

In our times a special obligation binds us to make ourselves the neighbor of absolutely every other person, and of actively helping him when he comes across our path, whether he be an old person abandoned by all, a foreign laborer unjustly looked down upon, a refugee, a child born of an unlawful union and wrongly suffering from a sin he did not commit, or a hungry person who disturbs our conscience by recalling the voice of the Lord: "As long as you did it for one of

POVERTY: DO IT JUSTICE!

these, the least of my brethren, you did it for me." (*Pastoral Constitution on the Church in the Modern World*, Vatican II, 1965, 27)

This (solidarity) is not a feeling of vague compassion or shallow distress at the misfortunes of so many people, both near and far. On the contrary, it is a firm and persevering determination to commit oneself to the common good; that is to say, to the good of all and of each individual because we are all really responsible for all...the stronger and richer nations must have a sense of moral responsibility for the other nations, so that a real international system may be established which will rest on the equality of all peoples and on the necessary respect for their legitimate differences. The economically weaker countries, or those still at subsistence level, must be enabled, with the assistance of other peoples and of the international community, to make a contribution of their own to the common good with their treasures of humanity and culture, which otherwise would be lost forever. (*On Social Concerns*, Pope John Paul II, 1987, 38-39)

Neither individuals nor nations should regard the possession of more and more goods as the ultimate objective. Every kind of progress is a two-edged sword. It is necessary if man is to grow as a human being; yet it can also enslave him, if he comes to regard it as the supreme good and cannot look beyond it. When this happens, men harden their hearts, shut out others from their minds and gather together solely for reasons of self-interest rather than out of friendship; dissension and disunity follow soon after. Thus the exclusive pursuit of material possessions prevents man's growth as a human being and stands in opposition to his true grandeur. (*The Development of Peoples*, Pope Paul VI, 1967, 19)

Preventing nuclear war is a moral imperative; but the avoidance of war, nuclear or conventional, is not a sufficient conception of international relations today. Nor does it exhaust the content of Catholic teaching. Both the political needs and the moral challenge of our time require a positive conception of peace, based on the vision of a first world order. Pope Paul VI summarized classical Catholic teaching in his encyclical, *The Development of Peoples*: "Peace cannot be limited to a mere absence of war, the result of an ever precarious balance of forces. No, peace is something built up day after day, in the pursuit of an order intended by God, which implies a more perfect form of justice among men and women." (*The Challenge of Peace*, NCCB, 1983, 234)

R-5 *THY WILL BE DONE: A WORD OF WITNESS*

Description of Activity:

Speaker or panel presentation on the Church's involvement in works of charity and justice.

Objective:

To explore how the Church responds to the needs of the poor on the local level; to meet those who work in direct service with the poor or speak out on their behalf.

Time:

45-60 minutes.

Materials:

Paper, pens/pencils.

Prior to the Activity:

Contact local church agency to arrange for visit or speaker; gather materials.

Procedure

1. Introduce the topic of the Church's active response to poverty and injustice, referencing the earlier *Involvement* and *Exploration* activities.

2. Brainstorm the kinds of responses people can make when faced with need. For example, learning more about the situation so we'll know where our energy will be most helpful; giving direct service to alleviate immediate suffering and respond to pressing needs; helping people to take control of their own lives and to change the situations that have hurt them; standing up for the dignity of those in need; and organizing to change the political or economic systems that deny their dignity. Indicate that seldom is any single response enough. Most often a combination of the responses listed is needed to change the situations that treat people unjustly or make it difficult for them to live and grow normally.

3. Introduce the speaker(s). Ask that they share: the kind of work with which they're involved and how it responds to the needs of people locally; why they're personally involved in this work/ministry; what the people they work with are like; what role they think the church should play in this and other situations of injustice; how other interested people can get involved in their ministry. Following brief presentation(s), invite group members to ask questions or respond to what they've heard.

R-6 *PREPARING AND PRAYING*

Description of Activity:

Preparing a simple prayer service around the issues of domestic/global poverty and hunger.

Objectives:

To reflect on Scripture and Church teaching as they impact the specific issues of poverty and hunger; to demonstrate the need to unite action with reflection and prayer.

Time:

40-60 minutes.

Materials:

Theme — appropriate prayer environment items, *The Scriptures Speak on Justice* and *The Church Speaks on Justice* resource sheets, *Sharing Good News in Prayer* resource sheet, music resources, other equipment as available/needed.

Prior to the Activity:

Gather materials. duplicate *Scriptures Speak*, *Church Speaks* and *Sharing Good News* sheets for distribution to group members.

Procedure

1. Introduce the topic of responding as Christians to poverty and hunger, referencing the earlier *Involvement* and *Exploration* activities.

2. Distribute the *Church Speaks* and *Scriptures Speak* resource sheets, asking the group to read individually through the sheets and identify a passage or quote that speaks to the issues they've been discussing. Share the passages/quotes and why they were chosen.

3. Invite the group to move into prayer around the issue they've been exploring, making prayer their own through active involvement in prayer planning.

a) With the group, identify a one-sentence theme statement for the prayer service that reflects what the group has heard and discovered.

b) Distribute and discuss the *Sharing the Good News in Prayer* resource sheet. Identify the different components of the prayer service and the possible ways people can be involved in preparing for prayer.

c) Divide the group into work teams to prepare: Environment/Art, Readings, Music, Gathering and Shared Prayer, Movement/Gesture, etc. Share available resources with the appropriate work teams. Coordinate the work of the different work teams to guarantee that there is a good balance and flow to the prayer service.

d) Share the Good News in prayer.

SHARING GOOD NEWS IN PRAYER

Jesus' Good News wasn't just for yesterday. It's also for today. And for tomorrow. Community prayer helps us keep the Good News alive in our lives. It helps us to "re-member" ourselves, to reconnect as members of the one Body of Christ. Prayer helps us to focus our vision and gives us strength to risk living fully.

The following is a basic format that can be used in designing a simple community prayer service.

A. Opening Song

B. Welcome and Statement of Theme

C. Gathering Prayer

D. Reading(s)

1. Possible sources for readings are the New Testament/Christian Scriptures; Old Testament/Hebrew Scriptures; Church documents; stories, poems or other readings which reflect the theme chosen and help people reflect on the Good News from a new perspective.

2. If more than one reading is used, it is best to separate them with a moment of silence, a psalm response, or quiet music.

E. Quiet Reflection

F. Sharing Our Understanding of Good News Today

1. Sharing can be done by one or two people who have taken the time to prepare their thoughts in advance.

2. Sharing can also be opened up to everyone in the group after a brief, prepared introduction.

G. Shared Prayer

1. Prayers of Thanksgiving or Petition.

2. Litany of Praise.

H. The Lord's Prayer or Glory to God

I. Greeting of Peace and/or Shared Blessing

J. Closing Song

Description of Activity:

Developing an advertising campaign to spread the good news of the Church's social teaching.

Objective:

To understand the principle themes of Catholic Social Teaching and explore their application to contemporary issues.

Time:

30-45 minutes.

Materials:

Newsprint, markers, paper, pens/pencils, *Basic Themes of Catholic Social Teaching* resource sheet.

Prior to the Activity:

Gather materials, duplicate *Basic Themes* for distribution to group members.

Procedure

1. Introduce the topic of Church teaching on issues of social justice, referencing the earlier *Involvement* and *Exploration* activities.

2. Distribute the *Basic Themes* resource sheet. Briefly discuss the six themes, noting the relevance and implications of each for the justice issues you have been exploring.

3. Divide the group into teams of 4-6. Share simple directions for their team task: Each team represents an advertising firm charged with the task of "selling" the Church's social teaching — helping people become more aware and moving them to action. The team is in the process of designing a full-page ad that will run in local newspapers or in national magazines targeted at different audiences. How would they design their ad to help people see the good news of the Church's social teaching in a new way? To show that the good news really is good? What symbols or illustrations, slogans or sayings would be appropriate? Assign, or ask each team to choose, a basic theme for its group work. Ask teams to develop a full-color draft of their ad on the newsprint provided.

4. Have each design team present its ad, explaining how it reflects the basic theme they chose to work with. Ask people to share any insights or learnings gained through their advertising assignment.

Source: The *Basic Themes of Catholic Social Teaching* are taken from *A Century of Social Teaching: a Common Heritage, a Continuing Challenge* by the National Conference of Catholic Bishops (Washington D.C.: USCC Office of Publishing, 1990) and used with permission.

BASIC THEMES
OF CATHOLIC SOCIAL TEACHING

Our Catholic Social Teaching is more than a set of documents. It is a living tradition of thought and action. The Church's social vision has developed and grown over time, responding to changing circumstances and emerging problems — including developments in human work, new economic questions, war and peace in a nuclear age, and poverty and development in a shrinking world. While the subjects have changed, some basic principles and themes have emerged within this tradition:

A. The Life and Dignity of the Human Person

In the Catholic social vision, the human person is central, the clearest reflection of God among us. Each person possesses a basic dignity which comes from God, not from any human quality or accomplishment, not from race or gender, age or economic status. The test of every institution or policy is whether it enhances or threatens human life and human dignity. We believe people are more important than things.

B. The Rights and Responsibilities of the Human Person

Flowing from our God-given dignity, each person has basic rights and responsibilities. These include the right to freedom of conscience and religious liberty, to raise a family, to immigrate, to live free from unfair discrimination, and to have a share of earthly goods sufficient for oneself and one's family. People have a fundamental right to life and to those things which make life truly human — food, clothing, housing, health care, education, security, social services, and employment. Corresponding to these rights are duties and responsibilities — to one another, to our families and to the larger society, to respect the rights of others, and to work for the common good.

C. The Call to Family, Community, and Participation

The human person is not only sacred but social. We realize our dignity and rights in relationship with others, in community. No community is more central than the family; it needs to be supported, not undermined. It is the basic cell of society and the state has an obligation to support the family. The family has major contributions to make in addressing questions of social justice. It is where we learn and act on our values. What happens in the family is at the basis of a truly human social life. We also have the right and responsibility to participate in and contribute to the broader communities in society. The state and other institutions of political and economic life, with both their limitations and obligations, are instruments to protect the life, dignity, and rights of the person, promote the well-being of our families and communities, and pursue the common good. Catholic Social Teaching does offer clear guidance on the role of government. When basic human needs are not being met by private initiative, then people must work through their government at appropriate levels to meet those needs. A central test of political, legal, and economic institutions is what they do *to* people, what they do *for* people, and how people *participate* in them.

D. The Dignity of Work and the Rights of Workers

Work is more than a way to make a living; it is an expression of our dignity and a form of continuing participation in God's creation. People have the right to decent and productive work, to decent and fair wages, to private property and economic initiative. Workers have the strong support of the Church in forming and joining union and worker associations of their choosing in the exercise of their dignity and rights. In Catholic teaching, the economy exists to serve people, not the other way around.

E. The Option for the Poor and Vulnerable

Poor and vulnerable people have a special place in Catholic Social Teaching. A basic moral test of a society is how its most vulnerable members are faring. This is not a new insight; it is the lesson of the Parable of the Last Judgment (Mt 25). Our tradition calls us to put the needs of the poor and vulnerable first. As Christians, we are called to respond to the needs of all our sisters and brothers, but those with the greatest needs require the greatest response. We must seek creative ways to expand the emphasis of our nation's founders on individual rights and freedom by extending democratic ideals to economic life and thus insure that the basic requirements for life with dignity are accessible to all.

F. Solidarity

We are one human family, whatever our national, racial, ethnic, economic, and ideological differences. We are our brothers' and sisters' keepers. In a linked and limited world, our responsibilities to one another cross national and other boundaries. Violent conflict and the denial of dignity and the rights to people anywhere on the globe diminish each of us. This emerging theme of solidarity, so strongly articulated by Pope John Paul II, expresses the core of the Church's concern for world peace, global development, environment, and international human rights. It is the contemporary expression of the traditional Catholic image of the "Mystical Body." "Loving our neighbor" has global dimensions in an interdependent world.

Description of Activity:

Developing a one-page summary of "The U.S. Economy and Developing Nations" (*Economic Justice for All*, 251-294) and applying it to the situation of farm and factory workers in developing countries.

Objective:

To explore the implications of economic justice for international and transnational business practices.

Time:

60-90 minutes.

Materials:

Paper, pens/pencils, copies of the Economics Pastoral or *U.S. Economy and Developing Nations* resource sheets.

Prior to the Activity:

Gather materials, duplicate *U.S. Economy and Developing Nations* resource sheets for distribution to group members.

Procedure

1. Introduce the topic of Church teaching on the issue of U.S. economy and its implications for international and transnational business practices. Connect this topic with the earlier *Involvement* and *Exploration* activities.

2. Distribute the *U.S. Economy and Developing Nations* resource sheet. Note that the sheets are a summary of just one part of a pastoral letter titled *Economic Justice for All,* published by the Catholic Bishops of the United States in 1986. Ask the group to read the selection individually, noting any words or phrases they don't fully understand.

3. Respond to any questions the group may have about the reading.

4. Divide the group into teams of 4-6. Ask each team to develop a one-page summary of the main points included in the reading. Ask them, too, to list the implications of the reading for the situation they've been exploring as a group — the treatment of farm or factory workers by international companies. How might international business practices and the situation of factory or farm workers change if the bishops' document was accepted as the basis for international business relations?

Source: *U.S. Economy and Developing Nations* is taken from *Economic Justice for All* by the National Conference of Catholic Bishops (Washington, DC: USCC Office of Publishing, 1986) and is used with permission.

THE U.S. ECONOMY
AND THE
DEVELOPING NATIONS:
COMPLEXITY, CHALLENGE, & CHOICES

1. The Complexity of Economic Relations in an Interdependent World

251-252. The global economy is the framework for the international solidarity we seek. We are concerned that U.S. relations with *all* nations be marked by fairness, mutual respect, and the values of Catholic teaching: human dignity; the unity of the human family; the universal purpose of the earth's goods; pursuit of the international common good; and distributive justice. But, because of our preferential option for the poor, we are focusing on U.S. relations with the Third World. There we must try consciously to protect human dignity, foster solidarity, and eliminate "the scandal of the shocking inequality between the rich and the poor."

253. Developing countries often feel dependent on industrial nations (especially the U.S.) for prices, financing, standards of economic behavior of foreign investors, aid conditions, etc. Northern advertising and media are increasingly penetrating their cultures.

254. Church teaching takes on new moral urgency as we understand: 2 1/2 billion people live in countries with an annual per capita income of $400 or less; at least 800 million there live in poverty "beneath any rational definition of human decency"; 1/2 billion are chronically hungry despite abundant harvests worldwide; 15 of every 100 children there die before the age of five. Their misery results from human decisions and institutions.

255-257. The interplay of individual nations, multilateral institutions, and transnational corporations and banks (along with many lesser actors) sets the context for policy choices. We need rules — especially to reconcile profit orientation with the common good. Interdependence erases the line between domestic and foreign policy, posing new factual and moral questions.

2. The Challenge of Catholic Social Teaching

258. Our moral perspectives have important implications: (1) *Love* and *solidarity* demand policies that transcend national sovereignty. (2) *Basic justice* requires that all peoples be able to participate in the global economy with freedom and dignity. (3) *Respect for human rights* (political and economic) requires we all seek a new global order where decisions, institutions, and policies are shaped by values that are more than economic. (4) *The special place of the poor* makes meeting the basic needs of the world's deprived and hungry the number one goal of international policy.

259-260. These perspectives call for fundamental reform of the international economic order. We urge renewed dialogue between the countries of the North and South to reorganize economic relations more justly. *The preferential option for the poor is the central priority for policy choice.*

---

3. The Role of the United States in the Global Economy: Constructive Choices

261-264. We join recent popes in strong support of U.N. efforts toward an international political authority with the power and responsibility to secure the global common good. Without one, economically strong national governments must cooperate on policies that enable the poor and marginalized to participate more in the global economy. This will serve the interests of all. The tendency in U.S. policy to define development issues primarily in terms of the East-West struggle and "national security" must be resisted. The reluctant, adversarial role of the U.S. in North-South negotiations must change; the U.S. should lead in helping reduce world poverty. Urgent, immediate steps are needed in aid, trade, finance, and investment.

265-266. a. *Aid*: While still the largest donor, U.S. foreign aid now lags proportionately behind most other industrial nations. Unjustifiably, it is increasingly bilateral and more militarized. This gravely distorts priorities: the U.S. is holding down the funding of the institutions that focus on the poor and create less dependency. We need to support or help reshape these institutions. The U.S., once the pioneer in foreign aid, is almost last among the 17 industrialized nations in the OECD in the percentage of GNP devoted to aid.

267-270. b. *Trade*: Trade is central to economic growth. The preferential option for the poor demands fair prices for the exports of developing nations and fair allocation of the system's benefits. Trade policy illustrates the pressures: Third World access to markets conflicts with domestic job security. The basic questions: Who benefits from a policy? How can benefits and costs be equitably shared? The trading system should benefit the poorest people and nations and not lead to human rights violations. We also need much better adjustment assistance programs for U.S. workers and families. Our society can handle trade dislocations better than poverty-ridden developing countries.

271-272. c. *Finance*: The debtor-creditor relationship exemplifies both global interdependence and the rapidly increasing *dependence* of developing nations. The roots of the debt crisis are *historic* and *systemic*.

272. *Historically*: The Soviet purchase of the whole U.S. grain surplus (1972) and the OPEC oil embargo (1973) forced prices up. The banks, flooded with OPEC profits, pushed larger loans on Third World nations needing to pay these prices. A second OPEC increase (1979) forced refinancing and more borrowing at higher rates. Global recession (beginning in 1979) caused Third World export prices to fall, reducing their ability to pay their debts.

273. *Systemically*. The global system of finance, development, and trade — the World Bank, the International Monetary Fund (IMF), and the GATT — seems incapable, without basic changes, of helping debtor countries manage their situation equitably.

274-276. The scandal: The poorest suffer most from IMF austerity measures, the fall of export prices, the inability to import food, and natural disasters. We must meet the immediate emergency. The poorest countries need longer payment periods, lower interest rates, modification of IMF requirements that hurt the poor — or cancellation of their debts to governments as some creditors have already done. The better-off debtor nations also need to be able to adjust without penalizing the poor. This problem is systemic: lending policies and exchange-rate considerations are intensely political.

277. The international debt situation requires systemic change to provide immediate relief and prevent recurrence. The U.S. should help reform the World Bank, IMF, and GATT so that they represent Third World debtors better. Such reform is morally right and in our economic interest. High interest rates generated by U.S. budget and trade deficits make the situation worse.

278-280. d. *Foreign Private Investment*: We hope for increased foreign private investment in developing countries consistent with the host countries' goals. We encourage investments by small and medium-sized companies and joint ventures. Private investment can sustain or worsen injustices (e.g., perpetuating oppressive elites, exploiting workers, or introducing inappropriate products and technology), or it can help develop the people, systems, capital, financial accountability, and knowledge important to development. Governments should try to direct corporate activities toward the common good. We urge development of a code for transnational corporate investment that encourages both development and just distribution.

281-282. e. *The World Food Problem — a Special Urgency:* Aid, trade, finance, and investment intersect in all economic sectors, but especially in food. The U.S. must develop a food policy that contributes to food security: access by all to an adequate diet. From the command of Jesus to feed the hungry to the Eucharist we celebrate as the Bread of Life, the fabric of our faith demands that we be creatively engaged in sharing the food that sustains life with the hundreds of millions facing starvation.

283-284. Hunger points to poverty. People must be enabled to grow or buy the food they need. Small farmers are the key to long-term agricultural and food-system development. They deserve support and protection. The U.S. must increase food aid and launch measures to develop food self-reliance in food-deficit developing countries.

285-287. Population growth (often seen as a cause of hunger), planetary limits, and the truly human quality of life are issues of urgent concern. Although poverty and hunger are not simply the result of large families, we support the need for responsible parenthood. Family size depends on economic development, education, respect for women, available health care, and cultural traditions. Population issues require an overall strategy of integral human development that respects parents' freedom (*Populorum Progressio*, 37).

4. U.S. Responsibility for Reform in the International Economic System

288-291. The U.S. cannot save the developing world alone. Third World nations share responsibility. Yet, pervasive U.S. power brings the responsibility to serve human dignity and rights more. Instead of promoting it, the U.S. should try to reduce the arms trade and stop putting "national security" ahead of meeting human needs. The gap between rich and poor — people and nations — is widening. The U.S. should launch a global campaign for justice and economic rights to match our political democracy. To restructure for a more just international order using the preferential option for the poor will require great sacrifices, leadership, and vision. "America, which in the past decades has demonstrated goodness and generosity in providing food for the hungry of the world, will, I am sure, be able to match this generosity with an equally convincing contribution to the establishing of a world order that will create the necessary economic and trade conditions for a more just relationship between all the nations of the world" (John Paul II to President Carter, 1979).

292. These "economic" issues are, at root, moral issues. To pursue global justice and peace, *we call for a U.S. international economic policy designed to empower people everywhere to continue to develop a sense of their worth, improve the quality of their lives, and ensure a just sharing of the benefits of economic growth.*

5. Conclusion

293-294. All these issues are interconnected; resolving them requires difficult trade-offs. Many of our suggestions would be expensive, but so would failure to act on these problems. We must examine tax reform and cut military spending, for example, to make our budget more fiscally sound and socially responsible. The U.S. has the funds to meet our social needs. Do we have the political will?

R-9 *POPE FOR A DAY*

Description of Activity:

Development of an imaginary papal letter addressed to the youth of the United States and offering practical suggestions for involvement around the issues of domestic and global poverty.

Objective:

To understand that Catholic Social Teaching is still developing and that people's responses to injustice can vary greatly depending on their situation and resources.

Time:

60 minutes.

Materials:

Newsprint, markers, paper, pens/pencils, *The Church Speaks on Justice* resource sheet, *A Papal Message to the Youth of the United States* worksheet.

Prior to the Activity:

Gather materials, duplicate *Church Speaks* and *Papal Message* sheets for distribution to group members.

Procedure

1. Introduce the topic of Catholic Social Teaching, referencing the earlier *Involvement* and *Exploration* activities.

2. Invite the group to brainstorm the justice issues which they think need to be addressed locally and nationally. How would this list be different if it had been drawn up by young people 25 years ago? 50 years ago? How would it be different, even today, if it were put together by young people living in Central America or South Africa? Note that justice issues shift from place to place and time to time. Responses to justice also shift as situations change and understandings grow.

3. Distribute the *Church Speaks* resource sheet. Ask the group to read through the resource individually, paying attention to what the Church says about justice issues and how it calls on us to respond.

4. Divide the group into teams of two or three. Share simple directions for their task: You've just been declared pope — at least for a day! Give yourself a name, then settle down for your first assignment. You care about people, and especially youth. They're important to you and to the future of the world. Write a letter to the young people of the United States, expressing your care for them and challenging them to use their talents and resources to make the world a better place for all people. Suggest a justice issue that you're both concerned about, and offer some practical suggestions for how they can get involved. Tell them why you're involved in social issues, and why you think they should be involved. Be positive. Be challenging.

5. Distribute the *Papal Message* worksheet. Ask the teams to use the worksheet as a basis for their letter to the youth of America. When teams have finished their task, share the letters with the entire group. Save the letters for possible later use.

A PAPAL MESSAGE TO THE YOUTH OF THE UNITED STATES

My Dear Young Friends,

Imagine, my first letter as pope! And I send it to you because...

Our world faces many difficult challenges, I turn to you for help because...

Despite all the good things that you have going for yourselves in the US, even your land is not empty of injustice and inequity. A problem that touches your lives deeply is...

Is there anything can you do about this and similar problems? Working together, I believe there's a lot we can do to change this situation, for example...

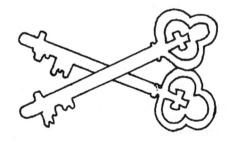

I feel strongly about these issues because...

And I know you feel likewise because ...

In closing, my dear young friends, let me assure you that God loves you very deeply, and so do I. Know that you remain close in my thoughts and prayers!

With much love and respect,

Pope _____

Date _____

ACTION ACTIVITIES ABOUT POVERTY AND HUNGER

INTRODUCTION

New experiences and ways of thinking lead naturally to new ways of living and acting. It is these new ways of living and acting that the fourth movement of the Pastoral Circle is all about. *Action* can take many different forms. In one sense, the *kind* of action step taken by an individual or group isn't as important as the fact that they're consciously *doing something* about the issue of poverty or hunger, taking a practical, next step on their justice journey. In another sense, however, the *kind* of action step taken can be very important. *Exploration* of the issues has helped us better understand the causes of poverty and hunger. We realize that hunger and poverty are complex issues. Real change will come about only when we work together to *alleviate the present suffering* caused by poverty *and* organize our energies to *eradicate the causes* of hunger and poverty. Working together, committed individuals can do much to make the world a better place for all God's people.

INGREDIENTS OF AN EFECTIVE ACTION RESPONSE

Any approach to *Action* should incorporate the following ingredients:

1. Action programming is most effective when it combines direct service with social change.

Christian action demands more than direct service. The majority of youth ministry programs emphasize direct service to help people survive their present crisis or need. Direct service rarely addresses the root causes of the problems. The strength of direct service is the face-to-face, interpersonal nature of the action. Working at a soup kitchen or food center, visiting the elderly or sick, and tutoring children are common examples of direct service. This is not enough though. Direct service needs to be coupled with social change — actions aimed at removing the causes of the problems that direct service is addressing. Social change analyzes the social causes of the problem and develops a response that addresses the injustice. Legislative advocacy, community organizing, and working with organizations that are changing the structures that promote injustice are examples of social change actions. Too often we overlook social change actions because we consider them too demanding for young people. Instead, we need to combine direct service and social change in the same action project. For example, young people who are working at the homeless shelter and soup kitchen could also be involved with the local coalition for the homeless which is working to create housing, employment, and just policies for the homeless. In this way young people will experience the benefits of working directly with the homeless *and* learn to change the system which keeps people homeless.

2. Action programming helps participants see the links between local and global issues and problems.

Not only should our service programming embrace direct service and action for social change, but we need to bring a global perspective to our actions. The most common problem with this ingredient is that

---

people always ask how you can serve people who are so distant. You can not directly. But by working through organizations which have a global a focus, like Catholic Relief Services and Church World Services (CROP), young people in your community can learn about people of another culture and country, as well as be in service to them. Most local service projects and justice issues have a global counterpart, for example homelessness locally, refugees globally. Hunger, poverty, racism all have local and global dimensions.

3. Action programming includes specific training for each action project to help people be more aware, comfortable and effective.

Young people will be most comfortable and effective in their service/action programming if they have specific information on the program or site and some basic skills training. Working with the elderly or the handicapped, organizing legislative advocacy, and participating in a hunger walk, for example, are very different activities that lend themselves to different kinds of advance training. Volunteer training is often available through the service placement. Be sure to check out opportunities for specific training when you contact the site.

4. Action programming builds on what's already happening in the community, utilizing existing programs and organizations.

Check out community, state, regional, church, and national organizations and agencies. Explore the ways in which the young people and adults in your local community are already involved in action. See what's presently happening ecumenically or what other church or temple youth groups are doing. There is no need to duplicate service opportunities that already exist.

5. Action programming is voluntary, offering participants a variety of choices about how and where they will work.

If Christian action is interesting, challenging, and exciting there is no need to mandate or force anyone to participate. Young people will want to serve. We will need to provide choices, so that they can select the project and when, where, and how they will serve. We must work with their schedules and commitments and not force them into our own convenient schedules.

6. Action programming matches the gifts and talents of participants with the requirements of specific programs and projects.

When you do your research on programs and sites, develop a profile of each project: (a) list and describe the placement/project; (b) identify the contact person(s); (c) describe skill/knowledge requirements and time commitment. This will become the basis for your orientation program and the choices young people will make.

ORGANIZING ACTION RESPONSES TO POVERTY AND HUNGER

The following process has been developed to assist you in organizing *Action* responses to the issues you have been studying with your group. The process incorporates the ingredients listed above and lends itself to a wide variety of *Action* approaches.

1. Explore Appropriate Action Responses

(a) Research Your *Action* Options: Organize your group, or a smaller planning team, to explore possible action responses. Read through the suggestions listed under the Action Approach categories found later in this chapter. List the action options that relate to the topic you've been discussing and seem like they could work for your group.

Check out the opportunities for direct service and social change available through parish, school, community, diocesan, and national organizations. Add any appropriate opportunities to your growing list of possible action strategies.

(b) Evaluate the Available Options: Now that you know the options available to you, evaluate them based on the needs and resources of your group. The ages, interests, experiences, and resources of the young people in your program will make some *Action* responses more appropriate than others. Some activities may fit easily into the flow of your program or academic year while others prove a tighter squeeze. Members of your school or parish community may already be involved in some programs, making peer leadership possible or giving you the opportunity to link the service involvement of youth with that of the wider community. Some service projects may demand or lend themselves to repeat involvement while others are one time experiences. Evaluate all of the options based on the criteria you have developed with your group or planning team to fit their unique situation.

2. Compile a List of Selected Action Responses

List and describe each of the *Action* responses selected by and for your group. Be sure to include a brief description of what each response demands of them by way of skill/knowledge requirements, preparation work, time commitment, etc.

3. Develop a Training Component for Appropriate Action Responses

Because your *Action* responses flow naturally from your journey around the Pastoral Circle, your group will already have a good sense of why action is needed. But that does not guarantee that they are fully equipped to respond. The young people in your group may need specific background or skills training to carry out some of the projects you've selected. These skills may be simple conversation starters or practical skills for tutoring or putting up a wall — whatever the skills may be, a concern for advance planning and training will make your eventual action response more enjoyable and effective. Often this training can be easily provided by the organization you will be working with or by local community members already involved in the project.

4. Present the Action Options to Your Group and Make Some Hard Choices

Present the *Action* options to your group, explaining briefly why this set of options was selected. Decide together whether you're looking for a single response to which the entire group can commit, or a variety of *Action* responses that allow for varying levels of commitment and availability. Balance, if you can, direct service and social change responses, as well as responses that take into account both the local and global dimensions of the issues studied. Select together, from the list of possible action options, several action responses that fit the interests and resources of your group.

5. Response Review, Specific Training

Review the selections made by your group. For any action responses that involve working with other agencies, check to see that the selections made by your group meet the requirements of the service agency and that the selections are compatible with the personalities of those involved. A young person, for example, who faints at the sight of blood shouldn't help with the bloodmobile even if all his/her friends will be working there. Provide preparation and training for any site that necessitates it. Make sure that everyone understands the project schedules and knows where to go for direction or support.

6. Action Involvement

If people are properly prepared and supported, and if there's regular contact with the service agencies involved in your *Action* response, the *Action* step of the Pastoral Circle should prove easy. If your group is involved in a service project that is a one-time commitment for them, the involvement of already-experienced community members (peer or other) in the project makes it easy for interested first-timers to continue their involvement. If the project is an extended one, or if you're coordinating the overall service/social action program and can't be available for every session, keep in regular contact with the site supervisor or coordinator. Check on the comfort levels of all involved; if a site really isn't working for an individual, talk it through and, if necessary change it. Better a temporarily unsettling change of site than a permanent distaste for Christian service. Make sure that hope and joy are built into every action response. Tough experiences grow easier when they're shared and there's a chance to talk, laugh, and learn together.

7. Reflection and Evaluation

(a) Shared Reflection: As your group carries out its *Action* response, there should be opportunities for those involved to reflect on what they're experiencing and learning from the project. Share experiences on several levels: what they saw and heard, thought and felt during their action response or service involvement; what they have learned about themselves, about those with whom they are working, and about the agencies with which they are working. Such reflection may suggest topics for later consideration or new training needs.

(b) Theological Reflection and Prayer: *Action* responses should lead participants to reflect once again on why they are involved in Christian service and social action. It should lead, too, to prayer: thanksgiving for unique personalities and abilities, new experiences and relationships; petition for newly discovered needs; praise for God's presence and assistance. New growth and learning lead naturally to prayer.

(c) Evaluation: As their *Action* involvements come to a close, engage your group in a systematic evaluation of their experience. Listen to their suggestions for change and improvement, curtailment, or expansion of the projects and activities with which they have been involved, Connect their *Action* responses with the *Involvement, Exploration,* and *Refection* activities that led up to it. Reflect again on the linkage with Scripture and Church teaching, justice awareness and social analysis. Often their suggestions provide a natural reentry point for another journey around the Pastoral Circle.

A-1 ACTION APPROACH: GROWING IN AWARENESS

Description:

Expanding present understandings of justice issues, concentrating particularly on the causes of injustice, the structures that keep it in place, and the *Action* steps possible to alleviate suffering and eradicate its causes.

Action Strategies

Personal

(What I can do individually to grow in awareness of poverty and hunger)

1. Take part in another program like the one you have just finished, building on what you have already learned.

2. Make a regular commitment to reading the newspaper or a weekly news publication like *TIME* magazine.

3. Be attentive to how the poor are characterized by the news and entertainment media.

4. Select an article or book from the bibliography, get it, and read it.

5. Subscribe to a magazine that deals with poverty or justice issues, for example:

Food Monitor	*Seeds*	*Sojourners*
261 West 35th St. #1402	222 East Lake Drive	Box 29272
New York, NY 10001	Decatur, GA 30030	Washington, DC 20017

6. Watch a "values video," a video that focuses on a social justice theme.

7. Write to a pen pal from another part of the country or globe.

8. Visit local agencies that work with the poor, hungry, and homeless to find out more about their operation and individual volunteer opportunities.

9. Take part in a multicultural or international festival or program; contact parish, school, and community leaders to find out about local opportunities and events.

Communal/Social

(What we can do as members of a family, parish, work, or school community or justice action group to increase awareness of poverty and hunger issues)

1. Share what you have learned with your family and friends.

2. Develop an education program on the issue you have been exploring to share with your parish or school community.

3. Add "information nuggets" to school/parish/community newspapers on the topic you've been exploring. A sample "nugget" could look like this:

DID YOU KNOW: Every day in the U.S.A., one in four children under 12 run short of food; most at risk are families headed by women with incomes less that 75% of the federal poverty level (Food Research and Action Center, 1991).

YOU CAN HELP: To help those immediately at need, contact _____ about making a contribution of food, money, volunteer time.

To help change this situation permanently, support *Children's Defense Fund*, a national action group that is working to change the policies and structures that hurt children and youth. For information on the *Children's Defense Fund*, contact _____ or write to: *Children's Defense Fund*, 122 C Street N.W., Washington, DC 20001

4. Give a friend or family member a gift subscription to a justice magazine

5. Visit local agencies that work with the poor, hungry, and homeless to find out more about their operation and volunteer opportunities for families or groups

6. Watch a "values video" together, then discuss it

7. Sponsor a school- or parish-wide hunger awareness week to provide people with the information they need to move into action

8. Support the work of domestic and global groups intent on educating people about the situation and needs of the poor; a few examples of such groups are:

Bread for the World
802 Rhode Island Avenue NE
Washington, DC 20018

Catholic Relief Services
209 West Fayette Street
Baltimore, MD 21201

Church World Services
P.O. Box 968
Elkhart, IN 46515

A-2 *ACTION APPROACH: ADVOCACY*

Description:

Speaking out on behalf of the poor; using political and economic leverage to change the policies and structures that create and sustain injustice.

Action Strategies

Personal

(What I can do individually to speak out on behalf of those who are living in poverty or hunger)

1. Write a letter to the editor of your local/school paper expressing your concern about the situation of those who suffer from poverty or hunger; a letter written in response to a particular news item or story is most effective.

2. Visit, call, fax, or write to your town, state and/or national representatives; communication in reference to specific bills or proposals is particularly effective. (See resource sheet on *Writing a Letter to Your Legislator*.)

3. Join a march or political rally organized to speak out for the poor or show political support for pending legislation.

4. Attend a voters' information meeting to learn how candidates for elected office view the poor and how they will vote on their behalf.

5. Vote for those who support your values and beliefs.

6. Boycott companies whose business practices are unjust or who otherwise take advantage of the poor; let companies know you're taking part in the boycott and why.

7. Support companies whose business and labor practices uphold the rights of the poor, and let them know why you're supporting them.

Communal/Social

(What we can do as members of a family, parish, work, or school community, of justice action group to advocate for the needs of the poor, homeless, and hungry)

1. Write a joint letter to the editor; letters written by, or on behalf of groups are more likely to be printed.

2. Communicate with your elected representatives; letters written by, or on behalf of groups are more likely to get an immediate response.

3. Join or organize a march or political rally.

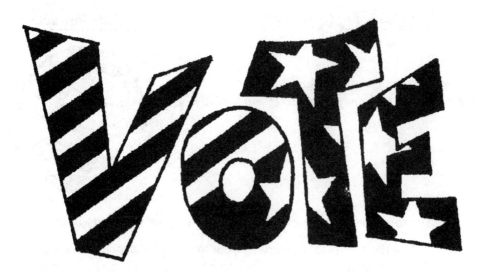

4. Organize a voter registration drive at school.

5. Develop, or make people aware, of candidate checklists, summarizing their statements on government programs for the poor and/or their voting patterns around these issues.

6. Organize a parish or school program and invite your elected representatives or candidates for public office to speak on the issue of government spending for the poor, etc.

7. As a family, parish, work, or school community, boycott unjust companies.

8. As a family, parish, work, or school community, support just companies.

9. Support the work of domestic and international groups who speak out on behalf of the poor; two examples of such groups are:

Amnesty International USA
322 8th Avenue
New York, NY 10001

NETWORK A Catholic Social Justice Lobby
806 Rhode Island Avenue NE
Washington, DC 20018

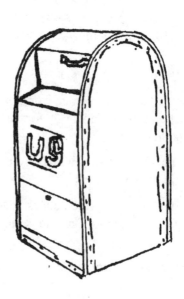

A-3 *WRITING A LETTER TO YOUR LEGISLATOR*

Whom To Lobby:

Whether expressing interest in a particular concern or writing about a specific bill, it is best to address your own legislator(s). Correspondence sent to others will generally be sent on to your legislator. You can request, however, that your legislator share his/her constituents views with colleagues, lobbying them for their support around the issue or bill you are addressing.

Where To Write:

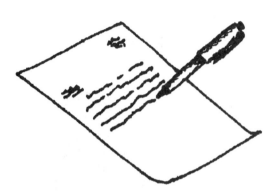

US Senator
The Honorable _____
United States Senate
Washington, DC 20510
Dear Senator _____

US Representative
The Honorable _____
House of Representatives Washington, DC 20515
Dear Representative _____

How To Write:

1. Be constructive — recognize that many of the issues legislators deal with are complex; everyone is honestly trying to do his/her best. Say something affirmative early on in your letter, e.g., thanking him/her for attentiveness to constituents or past voting performance.

2. Be focused — address a single, specific bill or concern; mentioning a bill by number makes it more likely that your views will be voted by your legislator.

3. Make the letter your own — personal, well-informed letters get a better hearing than standardized, photocopied letters. Share briefly why you are concerned and what experience or expertise you bring to the issue, for example, "Having discussed the issue in class and talked it over with my family..." or "As a regular volunteer in one of our town's soup kitchens..."

4. Ask questions that invite a specific response — make it difficult for your legislator to read your letter and send back a one paragraph letter thanking you for your interest. Ask for specific information, for example, "The bill assumes that ... " or "What evidence is there to back up this assumption?" or "How, specifically, would people in our state/district benefit from this bill?" or "A recent editorial in our paper suggested that ..." or "How are your thoughts similar to (or different from) those reflected in the editorial? "

5. Increase the influence of your letter — if you're writing as a member of an interested school, work, civic, or religious advocacy group, identify yourself as such — it will tell your legislator that you're not alone in your beliefs and make your group more visible.

Description:

Bearing witness to our concern for, and solidarity with the poor through a conscious effort to live more simply; modeling gratefulness and generosity.

Action Strategies

Personal

(What I can do individually to model in my life a concern for and sense of solidarity with the poor and hungry)

1. Fast on an occasional or regular basis; experiencing for a short time the hunger that many experience regularly, freeing up money to share with those in need.

2. Eat lower on the food chain; less meat, more grains and vegetables.

3. Contribute to parish and social agency food pantries.

4. Plant a garden and share your bounty with local soup kitchens.

5. Buy lower on the consumer chain; buying quality items while avoiding costly labels.

6. Buy fewer items; getting by with the "minimum we need" instead of the "maximum we want."

7. Support, with your purchasing power, companies that model just business practices.

8. Boycott, with your purchasing power, companies that model unjust business practices.

9. Share your time and talent generously with others.

10. Care well for the possessions you have.

11. Be generous with gifts, especially clothing; if a new item does not fit just right or isn't to your taste, give it as a new gift to someone in need.

12. Simplify gift giving; make your own presents or purchase them from crafts co-ops who share profits with the poor.

13. Share possessions, keeping major individual purchases to a minimum.

14. Make use of cost-free or low-cost recreational activities.

15. Share a generous portion of your allowance or work income with the poor; only you can determine what "generous" means in your situation.

Communal/Social

(What we can do together as members of a family, parish, work, or school community, or justice action group to model a lifestyle of concern and solidarity with the poor and hungry)

1. Take part as a family next Lent in Operation Rice Bowl, helping CRS aid the hungry of our world; for information on Operation Rice Bowl contact:

Catholic Relief Services
209 West Fayette Street
Baltimore, MD 21201

2. As a family, eat lower on the food chain.

3. Organize a parish, school, neighborhood, or work food pantry if one doesn't already exist; if it does, volunteer to help with collecting, storing, or distributing as a family or group.

4. Plant a family, parish, or community garden, growing what local soup kitchens need, preserving or canning the remaining produce for later use.

5. Buy lower on the consumer chain.

6. Use family, school, parish, and work purchasing power to support justice issues.

7. Regularly buy a family gift for one of the unknown poor who is brother or sister to you.

8. Swap names for Christmas and holiday purchases rather than buying individual gifts for everyone.

9. Share your family time and talents with others, opening your home to friends and those in need during the holiday season and non-holiday season as well.

10. Talk through family finances regularly; decide how and when major purchases will be made; decide together how much of the family income will go to charity and social change groups and how it should be divided.

11. Discuss, as a family, what financial security means for you.

12. Invest as a family or parish community in companies with just business and labor practices.

13. Examine your parish, school, or company budget to see how well it shares its resources with those in need; advocate for change if it's needed.

14. Become more aware of how your town, state, and country develop their annual fiscal budgets.

15. Read up on tough topics like the national and international debt, international tariffs and trade agreements — it's not nearly as complex as it sounds.

16. Monitor town, state, and federal budget proposals, attentive to how they impact the poor locally, nationally, and internationally; let your elected representatives know where you stand on budget issues and hold them accountable for their voting patterns.

17. Support the work of domestic and international "watchdog groups" that monitor the national and international responses to poverty, famine and health care; a few examples of such groups are:

Food First	*Oxfam America*	*World Health Year*
145 Ninth Street	115 Broadway	261 West 35th St. #1402
San Francisco, CA 94103	Boston, MA 02113	New York, NY 10001

A-5 ACTION APPROACH:
DIRECT SERVICE TO THOSE IN NEED

Description:

Working to alleviate the immediate needs and suffering caused by injustice; if direct service breaks down the social and economic barriers that keep groups apart, it can provide strong motivation to change the systems that keep injustice alive.

Action Strategies

Personal

(How I can involve myself personally in programs which directly assist the poor and hungry)

1. Research local service opportunities, looking for a good mix between agency needs and your talents and gifts.

2. Volunteer to work in a local homeless shelter, clothing shop, soup kitchen, or food pantry.

3. Clean out your closets on a regular basis, contributing good, wearable clothing to groups that help those in need.

4. Donate to a food or clothing drive.

5. Serve as a Big Brother/Big Sister to a child in need.

6. Tutor; serve as a literacy volunteer.

7. Sponsor a poor child or family in another part of the world.

8. Provide financial support to relief groups that work directly with the poor locally and globally; a few examples of such groups are:

CARE
660 First Ave.
New York, NY 10016

Heifer Project International
P.O. Box 808
Little Rock, AR 72203

Catholic Relief Services
209 West Fayette Street
Baltimore, MD 21201

Mennonite Central Committee
Akron, PA 17501

Communal/Social

(How we can get involved as members of a family, parish, work, or school community in programs which directly assist the poor and hungry)

1. Develop a listing of local service opportunities featuring practical ways that people can be involved as families or neighborhood groups.

2. Organize a volunteer service program with a local homeless shelter, clothing shop, soup kitchen, or food pantry (See introductory suggestions on *Organizing Action Responses to Hunger and Poverty*).

3. If your group is able to make a strong, long-term commitment, check with local social agencies to see if there are supplemental programs they'd like to have you organize/coordinate/staff.

4. Work with local supermarkets to cosponsoring a one-day food drive, turning over a percentage of the day's sales to local soup kitchens.

5. Organize a parish/school/neighborhood food drive.

6. Post an updated monthly list of items needed by local agencies in your parish bulletin, school newspaper, etc.

7. Provide financial support to missionary and relief groups that work directly with the poor, locally and globally.

8. Allocate a percentage of money raised through school or parish fundraisers for agencies that serve the needs of the poor.

9. Sponsor a poor child or family in another part of the world.

10. Twin with a parish/school in another part of your town, diocese, state, country, or world for selected social, educational, and prayer programs.

11. Sponsor a hunger walk or overnight fast program, etc. to raise funds to combat hunger (information on hunger walks is available from CROP; Food Fast from CRS).

12. Support the work of domestic and international relief and development agencies that serve the needs of those suffering from poverty, hunger, and inadequate health care; several of these groups are listed above.

13. Support national lobbying groups that push for stronger relief and development assistance to developing nations, for example

Institute for Food & Development Policy
1885 Mission Street
San Francisco, CA 94103

Interfaith Action on Economic Justice
110 Maryland Avenue, NE
Washington, DC 20002

14. Call, visit or write your national representatives advocating for increased assistance for developing countries.

A-6 *ACTION APPROACH: IMMERSION AND WORK CAMP EXPERIENCES*

Description:

An *immersion experience* is an extended (one week or longer) program designed to allow participants to experience day-to-day life and to understand the history and causes of injustice in another culture or country. While there may be opportunities for working with the poor, stress is most often placed on present growth in awareness as a basis for future efforts in direct service and social change.

A *work camp experience* is an extended (one week or longer) program designed to provide participants with an opportunity to work directly for and/or with the poor. While growth in awareness and options for future involvement may be part of a work camp experience, stress is most often placed on helping individuals and communities survive their present need. (For Action Strategies, see page 120.)

Personal

(How I can get involved personally in immersion or work camp experiences)

1. Start locally — grow in comfort and familiarity with the different ethnic and national groups that make up the population in your area; read about other cultures, listen to music from other ethnic or national traditions, explore new restaurants, take part in cultural festivals or events, etc.

2. Explore opportunities for extended or seasonal volunteer service in your area that reach out to the poor, homeless, and hungry.

3. Check with your parish, diocese, school, and local mission communities for existing immersion or work camp programs; learn about the experience and decide if you want to take part.

4. Write for national directories of lay mission opportunities; two excellent resources for adult and young adult opportunities are:

> *The Response—Lay Volunteer Mission Opportunities*
> International Liaison of Lay Volunteers in Mission
> 4121 Harewood Road, NE
> Washington, DC 20017   (1-800-543-5046)

> *Connections—A Directory of Lay Volunteer Opportunities*
> St. Vincent Pallotti Center for Apostolic Development, Inc.
> 715 Monroe Street, NE
> Washington, DC 20017   (1-202-529-3330)

5. Sponsor a friend or acquaintance for an immersion/work camp experience; provide financial and/or moral support.

6. Sponsor an exchange student from a developing country or take part yourself in a student exchange programs.

Communal/Social

(How we can be involved as members of a family, parish, work, or school community with immersion or work camp experiences)

1. Organize programs to help family, school, or parish members grow in awareness and comfort with other cultural groups.

2. Plan an alternative family vacation; experience immersion or take part in a work camp as a family.

3. Plan an alternative spring break; experience immersion or take part in a work camp as a school, parish, or friendship group.

4. Take part in an immersion or work camp experience sponsored by a local or national group; for information on immersion and work camp opportunities, check with your diocesan youth office or local missionary communities.

5. Organize an immersion or work camp experience for the youth or young adults of your parish or school.

6. Support the work of local and national groups that sponsor immersion, work camp, and extended volunteer experiences as part of their efforts in relief and development global awareness and cross-cultural understanding; a few examples of such groups are:

G.A.T.E. (Global Awareness Through Education)
Viterbo College
LaCrosse, WI 54601

International Christian Youth Exchange
134 West 26th Street
New York, NY 10001

A-7 *ACTION APPROACH: SUPPORT FOR CHANGE GROUPS*

Description:

Supporting organizations that work for change on the structural level.

Action Strategies

Personal

(What I can do individually to support organizations working for structural change around the issues of poverty and hunger)

1. Balance your charitable donations between direct services and social change groups; provide financial support for groups and organizations that work toward structural change around the issues of poverty, homelessness, and hunger; several examples of such groups were listed earlier.

2. Support the *Campaign for Human Development*, a United States Catholic Conference effort that supports self-empowerment and self-employment projects by low-income groups both locally and regionally.

3. Give a friend, family member, or acquaintance a gift membership in your favorite social change organization or gift him/her with a subscription to the organization's newsletter or journal.

4. Promote these groups with your friends, family, and acquaintances; pass around information on the organization, promotional brochures, newsletters/magazines, etc.

5. Check out the organizations in your town or state that work to change the structures that keep injustice alive — groups working to provide low income housing, homeless coalitions, welfare rights groups, etc.

6. Volunteer time with a local agency or organization that is working for structural change; their need for volunteers is as great as most other organizations that work to help the poor; check with Catholic Charities in your area for help in identifying such groups.

Communal/Social

(What we can together as members of a family, parish, work, or school community to support groups working for structural change around the issues of poverty and hunger)

1. In allocating charitable donations as a family, parish, school, or work group, balance monies provided to direct services and social change groups; provide financial support for groups and organizations that work toward structural change around the issues of poverty, homelessness, and hunger, such as those listed above.

2. Support the *Campaign for Human Development*, a United States Catholic Conference effort that supports self-empowerment and self-employment projects by low-income groups both locally and regionally; check with your diocesan *CHD* director to see what projects are funded locally, then support them with your time and money; for a national perspective on the work of the *Campaign for Human Development* or for information on *CHD* educational resources contact:

Campaign for Human Development
United States Catholic Conference
3211 4th Street NE
Washington, DC 20017

3. Check out local, regional and national organizations that work to change the structures that keep injustice alive (check earlier references in this chapter); put together a family giving guide that provides suggestions on social change groups that families in your parish, school, or neighborhood may want to support.

4. Consider alternative gift-giving patterns: enroll friends, family members, or acquaintances as members in your favorite social change organization; gift them with subscriptions to the organization's newsletter or journal; make a gift contribution in their name.

5. Volunteer time as a group with a local agency or organization that's working for structural change.

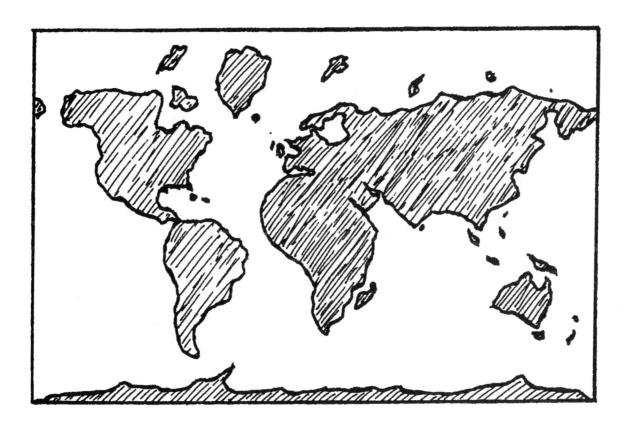

Description:

Understanding how choosing and preparing for a job or career relate to the Christian responsibility to alleviate suffering and work for social change.

Action Strategies

Personal

(What I can do individually to relate job or career choice and preparation to the Christian call to respond to the injustice of poverty or hunger)

1. Develop a list of the criteria you use for deciding on a job or career; how do the needs of the community and the call to justice enter the decision making process?

2. Ask adults you trust and respect how they mix career and Christian commitment, job, and justice.

3. Examine the steps you take in preparing for a job or career: training and course work, part-time or summer work sites chosen to gain experience around your career choice, etc. — how could these career steps be used to better equip you to work toward justice for the poor or homeless?.

4. Include an immersion or work camp experience as a formal or informal element in your career preparation plans; open yourself to ways your skills could be used in the wider world community.

5. Explore volunteer opportunities that allow you to use and expand your job/career skills; volunteer now.

6. Check out employment possibilities in both the profit and non-profit sectors of the job market; determine what changes, if any, you would need to make in your preparation/training to keep both options open.

7. Consider donating a year or two of your time, following school and/or training, to volunteer or lay mission work with the poor, homeless or hungry; prepare now.

Communal/Societal

(What we can do as members of a family, parish, work, or school community, or justice action group to relate career choices with the Christian call to respond to the injustice of poverty or hunger)

1. Organize a parish or school career night that helps youth, young adults, and others in transition between school and work to explore career options.

2. Introduce youth and adults involved in parish and school education programs to individuals who consciously live out their careers and professions in light of Gospel values, impacting the issues of poverty and hunger through their work and volunteer commitments.

3. Develop a parish, neighborhood, or work volunteer opportunity listing that helps match personal talents and training with volunteer opportunities in the local and wider community.

4. Establish a mentor or apprentice program in your community that links youth and young adults

with individuals who can share their career leanings and model commitment to justice in their lives.

5. Advertise in parish bulletins, school newsletters, etc., for short- and long-term volunteer opportunities with the poor and hungry in the U.S. and abroad.

6. Support, financially and otherwise, a parish, school, or community lay missioner/mission family.

7. Organize an immersion or work camp experience aimed at helping people explore the relationship between personal career skills and the needs of the poor.

A-9 ACTION APPROACH: INTEGRATING JUSTICE AND SPIRITUALITY

Description:

Incorporating justice learnings and experiences into how we understand and grow in our faith life, individually and as a community.

Action Strategies

Personal

(What I can do individually to integrate justice, and specifically the needs of the poor and hungry, into how I understand and grow in my faith life)

1. Define with whom you consciously pray as church: does your understanding of church reach beyond the boundaries of your parish, neighborhood, diocese, and country? Does it consciously include people of other cultural, economic, social, or religious groups?

2. Recall the people you have personally met or have read about, who live out their lives in service to the poor; consciously call them to mind when you pray, praying with them and for them

3. Read a magazine like *Sojourners* or *Seeds* that features individuals working for justice domestically or globally; include them and their ministry in your prayers

4. Examine what you pray about as church: what is the substance or content of your prayer? Are the needs of the poor, homeless, and hungry central to your praying? Does your praying reach beyond the personal and communal level to include national and global concerns?

5. Expand the content of your praying to include what is highlighted in today's newspapers or newscasts; clip out articles on the homeless and hungry; make those who are suffering today part of your daily prayer.

6. Consider the resources you use for prayer: prayer books and prayer forms, resources for spiritual reading, religious art, etc. Do the resources you use open you up to the reality of a universal and multi-cultured church? Do they help you image the many faces of Jesus — human and divine, suffering and resurrected, liberator from personal and structural sin, God of Europeans and Eurasians, North Americans and South Africans?

7. Find a picture, statue, or image of Jesus from another culture; read about Native American or Latin American ways of praying; listen to a tape of music from a Caribbean, African, or Asian church setting; purchase a book of prayer resources that features stories and prayers of another culture; see what difference praying from these resources makes in how you pray

Communal/Societal

(What we can do as members of a family, parish, work, or school community, or justice action group to integrate justice, and specifically the needs of the poor and hungry, into how we understand and grow in our faith life)

1. Explore how you define church as a parish or school community; how racially, culturally, economically mixed is your faith community? What attempts are made to reach beyond parish or school boundaries to the wider community? What is the level of participation in community, ecumenical, diocesan, and national programs to assist the poor and hungry?

2. Invite a member of your local or diocesan ecumenical council to speak about shared justice concerns and programs that assist the poor and hungry in your area; ask a missionary to share their experiences of working as church leaders with the poor domestically or internationally

3. Examine what you pray about as a community: what is the substance or content of your prayer? Are the needs of the poor, homeless, and hungry central to your praying? Does your praying reach beyond the confines of your parish, school, or neighborhod to include national and global concerns?

4. Expand the content of your community prayer to include the concerns of the larger church or wider community

5. Consider the resources you use as a family, school, or parish for prayer: prayer books and prayer forms, music resources, religious art, etc. Do the resources you use as a community open you up to the reality of a universal and multi-cultured church? Do the worship resources of your parish reflect the cultural mix of your neighborhood, parish, and diocese? Do religious art and images, vestments, etc., reflect a single- or multi-cultured vision of church? Are the holidays and holy days celebrated by your parish representative of the feast days and celebrations of parishioners?

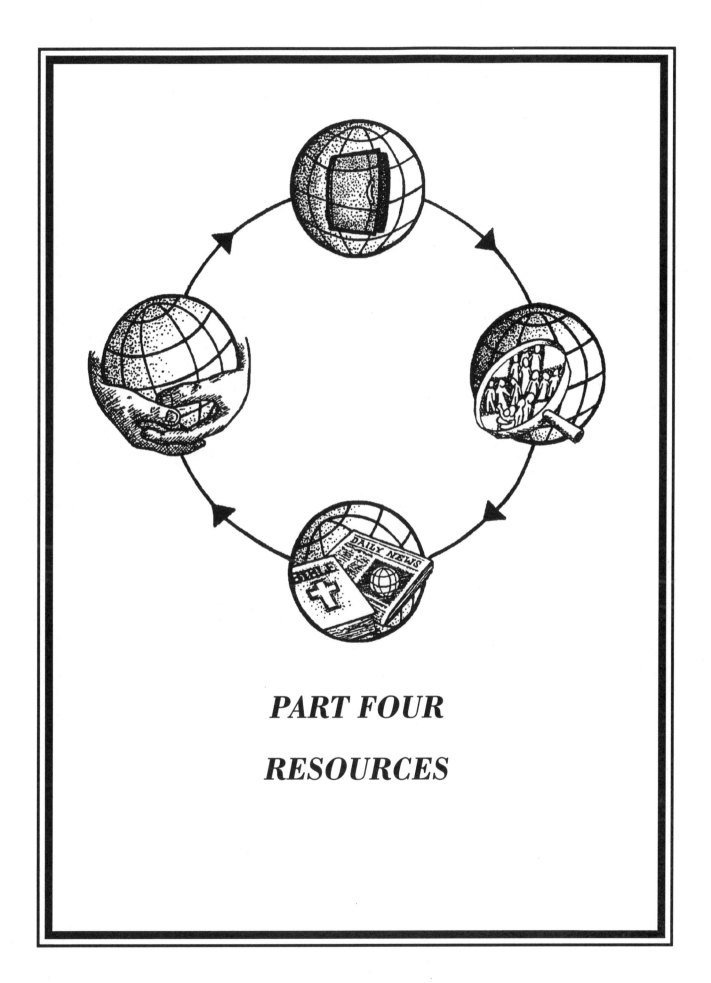

PART FOUR

RESOURCES

SELECTED READINGS FOR JUSTICE & GLOBAL EDUCATION

Foundational Readings

The Big Picture. Catholic Relief Services. Baltimore: CRS, 1990.

*Bright, Thomas, and John Roberto. *Access Guides to Youth Ministry: Justice*. New Rochelle: Don Bosco Multimedia, 1990.

*Holland, Joe and Peter Henriot. *Social Analysis — Linking Faith and Justice*. Maryknoll: Orbis Books, 1983.

*Morgan, Elizabeth with Van Weigel and Eric DeBaufre. *Global Poverty and Personal Responsibility*. New York: Paulist Press, 1989.

*National Council of Catholic Bishops. *Economic Justice for All*. Washington, DC: USCC Publishing, 1986.

Exploration and Social Analysis

*Children's Defense Fund. *The State of America's Children 1991*. Washington, DC: Children's Defense Fund, 1991.

Global Realities Fact Sheet. Catholic Relief Services. Baltimore: CRS, 1990.

*Guy, Kathleen A. *Welcome the Child: A Child Advocacy Guide for Churches*. Washington, DC: Children's Defense Fund, 1991.

*Holland, Joe and Peter Henriot. *Social Analysis — Linking Faith and Justice*. Maryknoll: Orbis Books, 1983.

*Lappe, Frances Moore and Joseph Collins. *World Hunger: Twelve Myths*. New York: Grove Press, 1986.

The State of the World's Children 1990. UNICEF. New York: Oxford University Press, 1990.(Available through: UNICEF, UNICEF House, 3 U.N. Plaza, New York, NY 10017.)

Africa's Food Crisis: Its Roots, Its Future. Catholic Relief Services. Baltimore: CRS, 1989.

Brown, Lester, et al. *State of the World 1990 — A Worldwatch Institute Report on Progress Toward a Sustainable Society*. New York: Norton & Company. (Published annually)

Czerny SJ, Michael and Jamie Swift. *Getting Started on Social Analysis in Canada*. Toronto, Ontario: Between the Lines Publishing Inc., 1988.

Ending Hunger: An Idea Whose Time Has Come. The Hunger Project. New York: Praeger Publishers, 1985.

Hofbauer GNSH, Rita, Dorothy Kinsella OSF, and Amata Miller IHM. *Making Social Analysis Useful*. Silver Spring: Leadership Conference of Women Religious, 1983 (8808 Cameron Street, Silver Spring, MD 20910).

Huntley, Alyson, Jim Morin and Marsha Sfeir. *Economic Rights and Human Development*. Dubuque, IA: Wm. C. Brown Company Publishers, 1984.

Justice and Peace Education Council. *Dimensions of Justice and Peace in Religious Education*. Washington, DC: NCEA, 1989.

McGinnis, James. *Educating for Peace and Justice: Global Dimensions*. St. Louis: Institute for Peace and Justice, 1984.

Our Common Future. The World Commission on Environment and Development. New York: Oxford University Press, 1987.

Williams, Sonja. *Exploding the Hunger Myths*. San Francisco: The Institute for Food and Development Policy, 1987.

The World Bank Atlas. Washington, DC: The World Bank (Published annually) (1818 H. Street, NW, Washington, DC 20433).

Reflection

*Henriot, Peter, Michael Schultheis, and Ed DeBerri. *Our Best Kept Secret*. Revised Edition. Maryknoll: Orbis, 1987.

*National Council of Catholic Bishops. *Economic Justice for All*. Washington, DC: USCC Publishing, 1986. (*Catholic Update* condensed formats of NCCB pastoral letters are available from St. Anthony Messenger Press, 1615 Republic St., Cincinnati, OH 45210.)

Hug SJ, James. *For All The People* — Summary of *Economic Justice for All* Pastoral Letter. Washington, DC: USCC Publications, 1987.

Kavanaugh, John and Mev Puelo. *Faces of Poverty, Faces of Christ*. Maryknoll: Orbis Books, 1991.

McGinnis, James. *Journey into Compassion — A Spirituality for the Long Haul*. Bloomington, IN: Meyer-Stone Books, 1989.

National Council of Catholic Bishops. *A Century of Catholic Social Teaching*. Washington, DC: USCC Publishing, 1990

Nelson-Pallmeyer, Jack. *The Politics of Compassion*. Maryknoll: Orbis Books, 1986.

Pope John Paul II. *The Social Concern of the Church*. Washington, DC: USCC Publishing Office, 1989.

Sheridan SJ, E.F. *Do Justice! — The Social Teaching of the Canadian Catholic Bishops*. Toronto: Jesuit Centre for Social Faith and Justice, 1987. (947 Queen St. East, Toronto, Ont. M4M 1J9)

Social Justice Encyclical Chart. NETWORK. Washington, DC: Network, 1989. ($2.00)

Action

*Guy, Kathleen A. *Welcome the Child: A Child Advocacy Guide for Churches*. Washington, DC: Children's Defense Fund, 1991.

Hollender, Jeffrey. *How to Make the World a Better Place*. New York: William Morrow and Co., Inc., 1990.

"How to Lobby for Just Legislation." Washington, DC: Network, 1987.

International Liaison of Lay Volunteers in Mission. *Let the Spirit Blow — The Response 1990*. Washington, DC: Published Annually.

Lewis, Barbara A. *The Kid's Guide to Social Action*. Minneapolis: Free Spirit Publishing Inc., 1991

NETWORK. *Parish Action Handbook: Legislative Advocacy*. Washington, DC: Network, 1987.

Office on Global Education, Church World Service. *Making a World of Difference*. New York: Friendship Press, 1989.

Withers, Leslie and Tom Peterson, editors. *Hunger Action Handbook: What You Can Do and How to Do It*. Seeds Magazine, 1988.

Resource Directories

Fenton, Thomas P. and Mary J. Heffron. *Food, Hunger, Agribusiness — A Directory of Resources*. Maryknoll: Orbis Books, 1987.

_____. *Third World Resource Directory — A Guide to Organizations and Publications*. Maryknoll: Orbis Books, 1984.

_____. *Third World Struggle for Peace with Justice — A Directory of Resources*. Maryknoll: Orbis Books 1990.

McGregor SJ, Mark and Mark Plausin, OSFS. *Examining Faith and Justice in the U.S. Economy: An Annotated Bibliography*. Washington, DC: Center of Concern.

* Asterisk indicates priority resource

SELECTED AUDIO-VIDEO RESOURCES

The Barrio Video Series: Charo of the Barrio, Bread for the Barrio, and *Messages from the Barrio*. Columban Mission Education, 1990. Each of the three units contains a video program and a leader's manual, lesson plans, Scripture background, activity/worksheets for duplication, background information, suggested resources and prayer services.

Bento. Maryknoll Video. The story of a young African-Brazilian who is determined to make life better for himself and his neighbors in a poor neighborhood of Sao Paulo.

Between the Times: The Catholic Bishops and the U.S. Economy. Washington, DC: Campaign for Human Development. 45 minutes. Study guide included. Purchase: $49.95.

The Business of Hunger. Maryknoll Video. Examines the relationship between cash crops and world hunger and offers an alternative vision of how the world's resources should be used.

Central American Close-Up. Maryknoll Video. The stories of four Central American young people: Jeremias of Guatemala and Flor of El Salvador (Tape 1); and Carlos of Honduras and Balty of Nicaragua (Tape 2).

Consuming Hunger. Maryknoll Video. Three videos on the role the media played in making the U.S. aware of the famine in Ethiopia and in shaping our response to it. Includes: Part I — *Getting the Story*; Part II — *Shaping the Image*; Part III — *Selling the Feeling*.

Down and Out in America. Explores the issues of poverty and homelessness in rural and urban America. Available from MPI Home Video, Dept. 1500, 15825 Robroy Drive, Oak Forest, IL 65402.

Heart of the Matter. Produced by the British Broadcasting System. Available through Bread for the World. Rental: $10. Using the Dominican Republic as a case study, this 35-minute video examines the causes and impact of debt on Third World countries and low income people.

Kenyan Youth: Preparing for the Future. Maryknoll Video. Three stories of determination, hard work, and dreams of a bright future from the youth of Kenya.

The Mouse's Tale. An animated cartoon from Australian Catholic Relief about a "fat" cat and a mouse (his conscience) exploring the issue of international food production and its relationship to hunger and famine around the world. Available from CRS. Purchase: $20; Rental $5.

An Overview of Economic Justice for All. Washington, DC: Campaign for Human Development. Purchase: $15.00

Refugees: A Call to Compassion and Solidarity. Baltimore: CRS, 1990.

The Richest Dog in the World. A creative, animated cartoon from Australian Catholic Relief which explores the plight of the world's poor and examines ways to effectively assist them to overcome their poverty and oppression. Available from CRS. Purchase: $20; Rental: $5.

Starving for Sugar and *Philippine Diary*. Maryknoll Video. Examine the past history of the Philippines and sound a call for a new sense of social responsibility.

PETERS PROJECTION WORLD MAP

This unique map seeks to provide a more accurate projection of the actual relative sizes of the earth's land masses and oceans, especially helpful in viewing the true size of the Third World. Copies of the Peters Projection Map are available from: **Friendship Press,** P.O. Box 37844, Cincinnati, OH 45237.

RESOURCE ORGANIZATIONS FOR ACTION ON POVERTY

Amnesty International USA
322 8th Avenue
New York, NY 10001

Bread for the World
802 Rhode Island Avenue, NE
Washington, DC 20018

CARE
660 First Avenue
New York, NY 10016

Catholic Relief Services/CRS
209 West Fayette Street
Baltimore, MD 21201

Children's Defense Fund
122 C Street, NW
Washington, DC 20001

Church World Service/CROP
P.O. Box 968 / 28606 Phillips Street
Elkhart, IN 46515

FOOD FIRST
145 Ninth Street
San Francisco, CA 94103

Heifer Project International
P.O. Box 808
Little Rock, AR 62203

Mennonite Central Committee
21 South 12th Street
Box M
Akron, PA 17501

NETWORK
806 Rhode Island Avenue, NE
Washington, DC 20018

Oxfam America
Educational Resources
115 Broadway
Boston, MA 02116

World Hunger Year (WHY)
261 West 35th Street #1402
New York, NY 10001